CONFESSIONS OF A PERFECT PARENT

Confessions of a Perfect Parent

W. Wayne Price

[handwritten inscription:] Patie & George — My dear friends! Wayne

WILLIAM B. EERDMANS PUBLISHING COMPANY
GRAND RAPIDS, MICHIGAN

Copyright © 1993 by Wm. B. Eerdmans Publishing Co.

255 Jefferson Ave. S.E., Grand Rapids, Mich. 49503

Printed in the United States of America

Library of Congress Cataloging-in-Publication Data

Price, W. Wayne, 1938-
Confessions of a perfect parent / W. Wayne Price.
p.   cm.
Includes bibliographical references.
ISBN 0-8028-0676-7 (paper)
1. Price, W. Wayne, 1938- . 2. Fathers — United States —
Biography.   3. Parenthood — United States.   I. Title.
HQ756.P73 1993
306.874'2'092 — dc20   93-19542
                                                        CIP

For
Frances R. Price

Contents

CONTENTS

Foreword: The Fable of the Unique Girl

JO ANNA S. PRICE

ONCE upon a time there lived a Unique Girl who believed in the myth of the perfect family. She believed that she would be able to make everything right for her children in spite of the fact that the family she was growing up in was not only imperfect but oppressive. Her house had barbed-wire fences around it. Black iron bars covered the windows. Every day Unique Girl dreamed about breaking through those confinements. She planned her escape for fifteen long years, from the first day she remembered peering through the bars of her baby crib. Rigid Mother had put her to bed for a nap. Unique Girl hated naps because she was energetic and curious, and the naps restricted her freedom. Rigid Mother had her rules, however, and Unique Girl dared not question them.

Unique Girl learned the hard way not to question rules. One day she learned that her brother had been

disowned by Rigid Mother and Angry Father. He had
been sent away to a far country, and Unique Girl didn't
know where he was. She missed him so; he had read
to her and held her on his lap. Now she realized that
if she did not follow the rigid rules, she might also be
banished to a far country. Unique Girl was afraid. But
she told no one of her fear. Instead, she resolved to be
good and perfect and especially to follow the rigid rules.

Much later, Unique Girl learned something about
her brother's fate. He had been sent to live with another
Rigid Mother, indeed in a far country. This Rigid Mother
was even worse than Unique Girl's Rigid Mother. There
were other Prisoner-Children where her brother was
sent to live. There were even more bars on the windows
and doors than at her house, more forced naps, harder
beds, daily assigned drudgeries, and weekly visits from
the Children's State Prison-House Inspector. Unique
Girl learned that if Unique and Creative children dis-
obeyed house rules, the Prison-House Inspector could
have them sent to an even worse place: the Regional
Prison Orphanage. It would be impossible for a Unique
Child to leave that place for at least ten years.

Fear of such a restrictive and punitive existence
caused Unique Girl to create another place to live. This
place existed in her fantasy world. There she created a
perfect and loving family. In this family, Unique Girl
could sleep when she wanted; she could eat what she
wanted; she could choose work that she could do well;
she could play every day. She could wear unique
clothes; she could run through the woods to visit the

neighbors; she would never fear being examined weekly by the Prison-House Inspector. In her fantasy world, children could play with friends as long as they wanted to.

Unique Girl's fantasy kept her alive. When Rigid Mother's rules and plans were too oppressive to bear, Unique Girl would pretend that she lived with the fantasy family who accepted her for exactly who she was. Perfect Mother would not demand obedience to arbitrary and oppressive rules, nor would she create unreasonable and difficult chores for Unique Girl to complete. In the fantasy family, Unique Girl would not have to clean out Rigid Mother's wine cellar at Rigid Mother's whim; she would not have to scrub Rigid Mother's goose houses daily, collect the golden eggs, pick the garden greens, or iron Rigid Mother's bed-clothes. There would be no weekly propaganda rallies to brainwash her. In her fantasy family, Unique Girl could think her own thoughts, ask her own questions, express her own opinions, read the books she chose, and play with fantasy-family paper dolls every day.

Unique Girl decided very early that she wasn't going to be like Rigid Mother when she grew up. She would be her own Unique, Creative Self. Rigid Mother was inflexible, domineering, and insensitive. Unique Girl would be patient, kind, sensitive, open-minded, gentle, understanding, calm, and considerate, just like her fantasy family members. She would teach her children love and sharing, she would tell them stories about other unique children, and she would laugh when they sang. She would never make them stay inside the iron fence, take forced naps, or perform daily drudgeries. Unique Girl's children could run in the woods, play with their friends, and bring other children home. She would take them across the Cultural Sea to visit the Museums of New Impressions. She would never make them attend weekly Brainwashing Rallies. She would never slap them with the Wet Dishrag or zipper them under the Locked Blanket that kept her in bed for naps when she didn't want to stay there. She would let them go to the Free Experiences Preschool that loved and accepted Unique Children like hers. Her children would never feel the humiliation and oppressiveness that she had experienced as a Unique Girl. Unique Girl's children would experience only joy, acceptance, and love.

Unique Girl did grow up and finally leave Rigid Mother's house. It didn't take her very long to find Accepting Boy. They fell in love, got married, and lived happily ever after . . . for twenty-five years. They loved their two little Creative Daughters to distraction. They planned and provided many wonderful educational experiences for them. They read them many fascinating children's books and encouraged them to have many playmates and friends. Their daughters were both beautiful and intelligent. No one else's children were so unique and happy or had such high self-esteem. Unique Girl and Accepting Boy had realized all of their fantasies. They were happy and pleased to have created the perfect childhood for their Unique Daughters. They felt proud, smug, and self-righteous, especially when they compared their experiences with those of all the Insensitive and Unenlightened parents they knew. Their family had the answers. After all, it was perfect.

Then Older Daughter arrived at adolescence, faced with the generational dilemma — to stay or to leave, to escape into a fantasy world or to reveal the iron bars and barbed-wire fences that she saw but that no one else seemed aware of. The decisions weighed heavily upon her, and her choices sent echoes and reverberations throughout the Perfect Family for many years. And her choices forced Unique Girl, Accepting Boy, and Younger Daughter to make certain choices. The choices meant either another escape from severe restrictions, or a cooperative effort at rearranging Unique Girl's fantasy so that all of them could help create a good world for themselves — together.

Preface

PARENTING has been the most difficult task I have ever undertaken — and the one for which I was least trained and prepared. Like many parents, I made the job too difficult by trying too hard and assuming too much. Having said that, I also want to say that parenting has changed my life in more positive ways than I could enumerate, has set me on a course of growing and learning. My daughters continue to teach me more about life and myself than all my formal education has. I am indebted to them both.

Perhaps, more than anything else, parenting has taught me a great deal about marriage, has forced me to do some of the hard work of learning how to relate better as a husband. Parenting is a lifelong task filled with implications for all other relationships!

Why should/would anyone write so personal a story? Three reasons. First, I wanted my family to be able to see in a codified and orderly document some of my own account of our personal and corporate struggles to change, grow, and learn. Second, I have the arrogance common to writers to believe that what I write might be read and be helpful or inspiring or educational to someone else. In fact, my story is not mine alone, not my family's alone; what I have experienced will connect with the experiences of other people. I hope that connection will contribute to their efforts to build and strengthen family and community. Finally, telling the part of my story contained in these pages has set me free from many griefs and regrets about my failures. It has become a public confessional that has enabled me to move forward with my personal, professional, and familial pilgrimages.

I am grateful to the three very important women in my life for their encouragement and support in this project. The book is a small tribute to them.

Introduction

IN the old days, the man paced back and forth in "the father's waiting room" while the expectant mother "labored" to bring forth their child. Occasionally, a "labor room" nurse appeared at the door to inform the anxious father that his wife was "just fine" and that "It won't be very long." The wait for the birth of our first child, Portia, lasted thirteen hours — grueling hours, as I was to learn later.

Shortly past midnight, I sent home the friends who were waiting with me. The rest of the night passed at an agonizing pace for both me and my wife, but for different reasons — in my case, ignorance, and in her case, travail. Just after the cold January light broke, this Sunday's child came full of grace. I held her and wept, praying the only real prayer any new mother or father knows: "God, I want to be a good parent!" Now, after the more humane birth of our second child, Jessica, and a couple of decades of such prayers, I suspect the best I can say is that I have been a mediocre parent, although I tried very hard to be perfect. I see it more accurately in retrospect.

Once in a while we parents stop, turn around, and gaze down those long corridors of experience. We seem almost startled by how clearly we see. Those decisions we agonized over, and some about which we were too certain to deliberate, all appear in a different light. Those events so vivid then now seem cloudy; the right and wrong, the good and bad, the confident bravado, the gusto of certainty coax a knowing grin when we look back at them. Other decisions, reached after such agonizing deliberations, seem almost self-evident in retrospect. Still other issues, so important or unimportant then, prove to be just the opposite from a more distant and objective vantage point. Hindsight may not really be 20/20; hardly any sight ever is. Still, the view toward the past is almost always embarrassingly clearer than our visions of what might be in the future.

Parenting by Choice

Essential to any retrospective is a more honest look at motives. Why become a parent? A century ago, such a question might have been moot. Modern couples, however, find it reasonable. After all, birth control enables most couples in developed countries to consider whether or not to have children, assuming they are physically able to do so, and to determine the number of children to bear. My wife and I were privileged to be able to consider the options. We asked all the questions — again and again and again.

A two-career, professional couple, we tried to frame clear and responsible questions. How effective could we be in parenting, given the massive demands of our work and studies upon our time and energy? Did we want to entrust a major part of the raising of our children to those we would pay for their services? Since we would be dividing our time between parenting and other responsibilities, we would miss many of the exciting events in our children's lives — could we accept that? On the other side of the issue, we asked about the desire to and the wisdom and advisability of setting aside one career. We never doubted our ability to live on one income; economics never played a part in the decision. But we believed that both of us had something to offer society through our professions. In our deliberations, we considered the possibility that becoming parents might even be a selfish decision.

During our first five years of marriage, we were certain we should not have children. Those were graduate-school years, a period of strange hours and wildly fluctuating pressures. The next five years would prove to be the ambivalent ones, with the emotional movement increasingly in favor of our becoming parents. The archetypal call to parenthood began as an echo and grew to a pulsebeat. Part of our compulsion was surely fed by the desire to create life in our own image. Such a need is part of our human nature — to create a being that is "ours," from us, like us. Yet, somehow my wife and I wanted to become better parents than we assessed our own to have been. I recall the words of a teacher who often said, "We are always improving on our parents, . . . but we never do!" I was sure we could — at least, I was sure most of the time! Although we didn't know it, the seeds of mediocrity were germinating. The pride that washed over our very motivations for becoming parents proved to be an illusion which inevitably grew into disillusionment.

During those times of deliberation, I struggled within myself to determine whether or not we had the skills and temperament that parenting required, or at least that our aspirations for parenting required. Such was my search for some formula, as if one really existed. Young and brash, I knew the weaknesses of my own parents; I tended to believe that whatever I had lacked in my childhood, I could provide for my own children. Whatever I didn't know, I could learn from other people, observation, and reading. So five more years and a great deal of discussion led my wife and me to choose to become parents.

Once we had made the decision, we set out to become the best parents we could be. We became observers of other parents and their children, carefully noting what we agreed with and what we would do differently. We began to read the standard works about the task of parenting infants. We attended Lamaze classes and considered the pros and cons of breast-feeding. We agreed that a new mother needed to be at home for as long as possible. That long, grueling process of decision making and preparation seemed to be reflected ironically in the long, grueling process of labor and delivery. But when Portia arrived, we were certain we had made a good decision, and we believed we were equal to the task. I felt unequal enough, however, to pray, "God, I want to be a good parent!" In retrospect, I believe a more honest prayer would have been worded, "God, I will be a good parent!" Who could fault such well-meaning determination! Who could fault such understandable hubris! But then, at that point, I was looking into a cloudy future.

The Best Seat in the Class

We human beings are inherently observers, learning by watching and mimicking others. As we grow older and become more sophisticated, we choose those we copy, those whose actions we deem worth emulating. Children learn quickly and easily from imitating the actions of others. When those children become adults, they continue to incorporate into their own behavior those actions of people they deem important. What parent has not incorporated into her own parenting tasks those methods she observes to be effective in other family units!

I became an observer of children very early. Since I was the eldest of six, it was often my responsibility to "watch the kids" while the adults were busy with other tasks. Much later, during two years as a public school teacher and throughout more than three decades as a pastor, the best seat in the class seemed to be in the front. Pastoral duties opened the doors of homes and the windows of the minds and hearts of dozens of families. The pastor was invited and/or welcomed in times of crisis, celebration, and change. I served as celebrant and official in the rites of passage: marriage and divorce, baptism and baby dedication, and a change of residence. I was privileged to hear intentionally verbalized joys and frustrations; I was able to interpret more subtle expressions of the rewards and trials of parenting. In both classroom and church I often listened to children and saw some things from their perspectives as they directed them to me or to anyone who would keep their secret. I overheard the children as they talked with one another or acted out their impressions in their work and play.

I became a sponge, soaking up everything having to do with families and children. The births of our children seemed to intensify my interest. Like most parents, I began to form opinions about children's learning processes, children's play, discipline, the formation of values, the place of religious faith in children's lives, food and mealtimes, reading and music. All of it was exciting, fascinating, and adventuresome. Perhaps the finest reward in those earliest parenting years was the opportunity I received as an adult to return to my own childhood and relive many of my own most pleasant experiences; I was also able to experience for the first time many things I had missed as a child. Music I had never heard before became a fresh inspiration. Books and stories I had missed were there for me to discover along with my children. Ballets, plays, parks, museums, toys, clothes — I enjoyed them all as though for the first time. I often felt like a child with my own children.

We all enjoyed reading. One indelible image re-appears to this day: Jessica approaching us with an armload of books, demanding, "'ead me a book!" We read books at mealtime, bathtime, bedtime, and in-between-times. We patronized bookstores and ordered books by mail. "What do you do with all these books?" our mail carrier once asked us.

We also enjoyed music. Portia and Jessica soon learned to operate a small phonograph and a cassette player. They sat on the floor for long periods of time playing records and tapes and singing songs they had memorized. Now, more than two decades beyond the beginning of my parenthood, I find myself singing those songs without missing a word.

My involvement with my own children and my observations of other children and their families seemed to intensify my love of these little ones and my original desire to be a good parent. Every responsibility seemed like a gift. I enjoyed mealtimes, bathtimes, playtimes, and holidays. I am sure I believed I was the first to have children. In fact, a dear friend commented in my presence, "Wayne thinks he's the only person who's ever been a parent!"

Yet for all the periodic euphoria of parenting, it is no perennial Disneyland. As children grow, they not only develop their own minds and wills but they also begin to acquire the tools to express themselves. Portia and Jessica certainly did so, and my wife and I encouraged that. We simply had no idea the long-term parenting process could be so difficult.

Hints of Things to Come

The difference between a mediocre parent and a really good parent is more than a matter of desire and dedication. In fact, parents can try too hard and fail at the very point of allowing, in Wordsworth's image, the child to be "father of the man."

I soon discovered that each of our children had more of an independent mind and disposition than I had expected. Portia was an extrovert from the beginning. She loved to be around people, disliked going to bed or otherwise being alone, and protested mightily the entire idea of her own room and solitude. Her mother and I spent many nights pacing the floor with this tiny crying child in no more distress than facing her dark and empty room. If we held her, took her to the family room to play, or otherwise put distance between her and her crib, she was fine. She brought more than a little change to two parents who were essentially private, quiet adults.

By the time Portia was six months old, I was aware that she did not share my plans for her or my expectations of her. In a family magazine I published a little piece called "Left Foot Forward." I indicated with some reserved pride that many of my daughter's characteristics were completely opposite those I had expected her to have. I expressed a great deal of pride in such an independent and willful child. She even liked spinach! If I had been as keen an observer of people as I thought I was, however, I might have recognized that her sense of order, time, learning, and play were also much different from my own. I was destined to learn the hard way just how different.

Jessica, four years younger, would bring still other distinctive traits to our reordered family. Portia's strong-willed personality tended to be suppressed by her desire to please everyone. Whatever her parents chose for her, she quietly set out to enjoy, but that old hindsight now tells us she was most often more interested in pleasing her parents than in exploring her own self and her world. Not Jessica! Right off the bat she plowed ahead with all the grace of a bulldozer. She crawled, walked, climbed, ran, explored, rummaged, and experimented. Wherever she went, a wake of flotsam and jetsam floated behind her. She too was telling us that she had her own disposition and her own mind. She was much more direct in the expression of her personality. She spoke that mind, shed her shoes at every opportunity, and homesteaded every territory in sight. No place and no thing was personal or private. She would be seen and heard; she would not be denied. She attracted to her those personalities who enjoyed children with independent spirits.

In her too I should have seen that no child is the sum of all her most immediate forebears. She was the bits-and-pieces product of many generations, molded into one unique individual. On the one hand, I was proud of her independent spirit; on the other hand, I was never completely comfortable with its relentless expression.

Both children from their earliest days sought to develop and express uniqueness; like all children, they were often torn between the need to live according to parental expectations and the need to explore what about them was solely their own. The result was a combination of fun, excitement, wonder, frustration, anxiety, and exasperation. In this respect our family was not very different from most other families whose parents are conscientious and committed to their tasks.

The difference between excellence and mediocrity, however, seems now to have rested in the fact that my wife and I were slow to adapt our plans and expectations to these little ones who were developing plans and expectations of their own. We were not always alert and flexible enough to notice the occasions and circumstances in which they responded with glee, ecstasy, and unfettered laughter. These are always clues to a child's sense of order, time, creativity, and even independence.

Mediocrity as an Improvement

The adolescence of both Portia and Jessica became a period of reassessment for our family. The enormous and difficult tasks involved in a child becoming an adult strained our family's self-image to the point of forcing my wife and me to question practically every motivation and method involved in parenting. We have been fortunate to have avoided the abuses of drugs, alcohol, and the law. We have been even more fortunate to have had the help of personal and professional friends who have journeyed with us. In fact, the process of re-evaluating our own parenting tasks has led us to the greatest step in personal and interpersonal growth: recognizing that our system was essentially flawed by too much pride and too little of several important qualities such as flexibility, humor, trust, openness, and humility. Confession of mediocrity may be an improvement over illusory perfection.

In the pages that follow I will deal with the period of adolescence as a crossroads for most families, and I will make some observations about how parents can prepare for the tasks of nurturing adolescents. In the next two chapters I will return to childhood issues as they relate to such preparation. In the remaining chapters I will deal with adolescence as a time for families to move into new and even more positive relationships.

In *Walden,* Henry David Thoreau commented that he wouldn't talk about himself so much if there were anyone else he knew as well; I can say the same. This is my story, the story of a serious, well-meaning parent who continues to learn from his children. It is the story of the pains accompanying discovery, the griefs brought on by many losses, the melancholy and regret of mistakes, and the self-conscious satisfaction of progress. This is the story of a person who at one time was nearly broken by the task of parenting, and who subsequently was strengthened precisely in the broken places.

Yet this story, I suspect, is not solely my own. In addition to being part of the stories of the other members of my family, it is also part of the stories of nearly all other contemporary parents. Perhaps most of us are mediocre parents, or think we are. And perhaps the discovery we most need to make is that our children will not ultimately succeed or fail on the basis of our excellence or mediocrity as parents. They too bear responsibility for what they become.

CHAPTER I

Who Is This New Person?

ANY strength, pushed to its extreme or greatly exaggerated, becomes a weakness. As ironic as it sounds, parents can try too hard, be too involved, accept too much responsibility. Most of us know at the far end of the parenting task how strangulating apron strings can be. We all know the stifling effects of smothering, offered in the name of love. We might argue about whether it is possible to love too much; we would not argue about whether the wrong kind of love — smothering, possessive, hovering love — prevents a child or any other person from reaching his or her own highest level of personhood.

At the top of my own list of confessions must stand such an acknowledgment. I tried too hard. I accepted too much responsibility for the personhood of my children. I was overinvolved. After all these years my daughters still say to me, "Dad, you can't protect me

13

from everything!" or "Dad, I have to learn from my own mistakes!" And how right they are.

Why Do I Need To Be So Involved?

The identity of the new person is separate from yet bound up with the identities of the parents, which have been shaped by their backgrounds. I know now, as surely as I know night from day, the source of my own overinvolvements. I came from a large family that in many ways was preoccupied with survival. Most important to us after the basic necessities of life were religious faith and church activities. Since I was the oldest of six children, my duties often came before play. Consequently, I grew up feeling enormous responsibility for my family. Birth order, family size, and economic necessities all tend to influence the kind of parent one will eventually become. Such factors may also create doubts about whether or not one should even become a parent.

I am certain now that my ambivalence about wanting to be a parent came from uncertainty about repeating a parenting task I had assumed as a child. In the clarity of hindsight, I now know my hesitations had even more to do with self-doubts: everything I remembered about parenting and childhood emphasized the difficulties and recalled little in the way of celebration. From early adulthood on, I could never completely convince myself that good (read "perfect") parenting was possible for anyone, or that I could be a good (perfect) parent.

My wife has her own story, and surely her own set of confessions, but she too struggled with the parenting issue from a different background. The adopted child of foster parents fifty years her senior, she experienced childhood as a struggle with her own identity and sense of belonging; she saw the role of being a child — in part — as a set of achievements by which she could earn acceptance. From her viewpoint as a young adult, parenting seemed like a task of protecting and directing a child — again, with little play or celebration.

From the moment we decided to try to become parents, we were committed to the impossible: perfection. Yet, I must admit that perfection was perhaps my goal more than hers. Whatever my own parents lacked, I would achieve through education, effort, and economic advantage. My own parents may have stinted on their gifts to me of knowledge, time, attention, training, and even commitment, but I would see to it that my child or children would have such available to them. I wanted to be a perfect parent and I would try, try, try — and succeed! At worst this is always a formula for gloomy failure; at best it is a rather heavy burden for both parents and children.

In their desire to do a good job, most parents at least lean toward a desire for perfection. Listen as we talk about wanting our children not to have to work as hard as we had to work. Notice how often we talk about working so our children will have advantages we never

15

had. Most of us want our children to know more, experience more, have more, and do more than children of our own generation. Given such high expectations, success is nearly always nonexistent or illusory, because anything less than perfection seems like failure!

A One-Sided Theory of Childhood Development

I became a parent believing that whatever a child becomes is decided outside of the womb. Genetic influences determine physical characteristics; home, church, school, and the child's own development determine what he or she will become. I would never have verbalized such an opinion, however! Even as I see these words in print, I cringe. Like most students of the humanities, I had always argued that the heredity-or-environment theories were too limiting. Genetic determinants must be factored into human personality; environmental effects are extremely important but not alone in their influence. The issue was less like either/or and more like both/and — in theory, at least!

Indeed, the progress in research in areas related to human personality, temperament, and behavior have carried the old heredity-and-environment issues to such new levels that the discussions in my college days now seem like light from kerosene lamps compared with laser beams. The irony lies in the fact that for the past two or three decades, I have read extensively in areas related to human personality and interpersonal dynamics. But theory is one thing; practice is another. In reality, I refused to see that my own expectations for myself and my children were flawed in theory and damaging in practice.

When the issue related to my children, I functioned as a parent from the perspective of parent-as-shaper-of-personhood. The children were not mine to own or to keep; I said that many times. They were destined to become adults, able to function successfully and in fulfilling ways without me; I frequently said that as well. Again, theory is one thing; practice is often another. In fact, I believed my wife and I were responsible for teaching these two children what they needed to know, for providing them with foundations of religious faith and ethics, and for giving them whatever tools possible to function as adults as we became less and less a part of their world.

Had anyone told me I was attempting to function in this way, I would have denied it. I am sure I would have offered in my own defense a firm opinion that my children clearly reflected their parents and grandparents in physical appearance and behavior. And I probably would have argued that I knew I could not override with training everything genetic. I would have admitted, however, to giving it my best effort.

What may be the most difficult aspect of arrogating to myself the role of shaper of personhood has been the theological heresy of such a direction. The grave sin of it all was my desire to make these children into my own image. I have long since repented of such. Both my

17

children and I bear the scars of my own ill-chosen theory and practice. And to their credit, they have been sufficiently their own persons to have resisted such efforts, even though the cost to family harmony has at times been high. To their credit and ours as parents, this struggle has been the single greatest building block in our growth as individuals and our progress as a family. The story of our struggle will become more specific in the pages that follow.

The Theory at Work

Having determined, then, to shape, mold, direct, teach, guide, and otherwise develop Portia and Jessica into full personhood, my wife and I threw ourselves into the task. Notice the word *task*. Parenting was often a project rather than a celebration or a journey or a relationship of grace. In retrospect, however, the process was not without both celebration and grace. All four of us would say that, taken as a whole, the parenting/childhood period was positive, although too often intense. But then, important "projects" always are.

As my wife and I reflect upon our activities, we smile in amazement that we had the energy to do all we did. We discovered that perfection requires enormous effort and energy. We helped found a Montessori school: I served as the first chairperson of the board and either my wife or I served on the board for many years. We helped to establish a mothers'-day-out program in our church, an all-volunteer effort that reached a participation level of seventy-five preschoolers. We accumulated a veritable storehouse of "educational" toys, a library of children's books and audio resources, and a rather fine collection of self-help books for parents. We attended workshops, classes, and study groups. So thoroughly did we throw ourselves into parenting that we must have appeared to have been trying to reform all the other parents in our community.

The children, the "objects" of our duties, were hardly exempt from the parent-imposed work of growing up. We dragged them to libraries, museums, cities, parks, monuments, beaches, concerts, stage performances, historical sites, college campuses, and religious meetings. One daughter now despises large cities. On a family "vacation," our other daughter — on crutches because of a broken foot — complained about the visit to the Statue of Liberty: "I don't see what's so special about this place; they ought to pay us to come here!" That cut like a knife, not because I suddenly realized the difficulty of getting around New York City on crutches and in the oppressive August heat, but because I expected her to have the kind of background — at age fourteen! — to understand the city's significance to this nation. The girls were under pressure to know, understand, appreciate, respond to, and celebrate these "advantages" according to their father's tastes and timetable rather than their own. I have thought since about another of Thoreau's comments: "Whenever I see someone coming to do me good, I turn and run in the other direction."

More revealing than any of us had realized is the most anticipated of our family traditions: our annual weeks at the beach. This has been, perhaps, the only time and event of the year during which the girls have been perfectly free to come and go, sleep or stay up, choose their activities, and simply be themselves. Not that they have turned from the cultural activities, books, and ideas that we have discovered and shared. They have continued to grow in their appreciation of them. Nevertheless, the beach has been more important to them because of the absence of pressure to follow their parents' — especially their father's — commitment to being "good parents."

Again, my wife and I should have assessed our efforts partially in light of our daughters' responses and reactions. But then, we were shaping them and not the other way around. Or so we thought.

Early Warning Signals

With that near-perfect hindsight, I recall two early hints our children offered that we were pushing too hard, were overinvolved. One indication came early from Portia. Before she was three years old, we spent one month in France while her mother was doing academic research. She and I spent each day touring Paris, playing in the parks and simply being together. The three of us spent evenings having dinner and enjoying more tourist activities. The trip was indeed good for all of us. Almost immediately upon our return, however, my wife and I enrolled our daughter in a Montessori preschool, the best we could find. Because she was an outwardly compliant child, her protests were minimal, and we were assured by the director that she would adjust. Externally, she did. But soon after enrollment, she began to bite her fingernails. I noticed it and ignored it because I didn't want to face any reality not consistent with the program. In fact, she was not happy with the additional structure such an environment brought into her life; she did not need to be in a school setting this early, and we would later learn more about the reasons. First early warning signal ignored.

Four years after the birth of our first daughter, Jessica appeared with a ready-made personality. We now smile knowingly when we talk about how she announced her presence in utero. She was an active child even before birth. When she arrived on the scene, she came with her own opinions, desires, and determination. She seemed to have her own sense of order, or to us, disorder. Whereas Portia had been apparently compliant and orderly, Jessica delighted in staking claim to every part of the house, primarily exploring and dumping things out. She picked things up only under duress. By the time she was three years old, it was clear that she was her own person and that any molding, shaping, and directing her parents might try would require even more determination. She brought with her the makings of a real test of wills.

Experts in the fields of child psychology and family

therapy frequently speak of "acting out," that process whereby children express through destructive behavior their inner reactions to their own adjustment problems or family dysfunctions. For example, a child may react to family tensions through bed-wetting, temper tantrums, or violence toward other children. Acting out is hardly limited to children, however. Adolescents may express their deepest turmoils through promiscuity, substance abuse, outlandish dress, and a variety of other dramatic behaviors.

Whenever issues and events threaten to overwhelm any of us to the point where we are unable to verbalize the depths of our feelings or find help, we turn to some dramatic actions by which we cry for help. Circumstances that children may not completely understand may increase their need to act out their fear, anger, grief, and even joy. Children tend to lack the verbal sophistication necessary to express dissatisfaction with events involving them; they turn to varying degrees of dramatic behavior. Such expressions may be as subtle as nail-biting or as violent as temper tantrums.

Neither of our children protested their situations with such intensity that our household order was threatened. In fact, ours seemed to be a well-adjusted, healthy family, and by any standard it would have been judged to be above average. In spite of appearances, however, our family was probably quite average. As parents, my wife and I were much less attuned to what our children were telling us than we now wish we had been. Both the girls expressed themselves in very subtle ways that deserved more attention than we gave those behaviors. Portia was trying to tell us she was uncomfortable with all the order we were imposing upon her. She needed to be free to explore, create, and socialize. Jessica tried to tell us that she simply was not going to respond to anyone else's demands. She refused to perform, answer, or reveal what she had in mind until she was sure she had it sorted out to her satisfaction.

On the one hand, signals from our quietly compliant Portia were easy to ignore when we chose to do so. On the other hand, protests from Jessica proved impossible to ignore. She chose to call the tune. Each day we asked her what she had done in school, or in Sunday school, or at a friend's house. If she wasn't ready to tell us, her evasive answer was a nonsense word: "Tooka!" Days later, on her own schedule, she told us what we wanted to know. As early as four years of age, she would make these revelations on her terms.

Jessica further struggled with her place as "the littlest rabbit." She recited stories, songs, or poems only when she was sure she could do them perfectly. She competed with the others in the family and felt the need to compete on level ground. I cannot soon forget her forlorn musings one day as we were riding in the car. "Daddy can read. Momma can read. Portia can read. (Pause) Everybody in this family can read but me!"

Our children very early felt the pressures of being shaped and molded. Each reacted differently, but each reacted. Their parents were terribly slow to read the nonverbal messages. Sadly, it is not unusual for many adults to overlook the clearest and most incisive messages their children try to send them. Parents may acquire excellent verbal skills, but we tend to lag far behind in the skills of listening and observing. If we hear imprecisely, we see through a glass darkly. Children always do their real communicating through behavior. Father does not always know what is best, and meaning well or trying hard may be little more than lame excuses for ignoring vital messages we deem inconsistent with the way we want things to be.

Children are not born as blank slates upon which parents write. Neither are they shapeless masses of clay which parents mold. Children bring with them a great deal of in-place personality; they develop in part along lines of their own choosing. I see that now much more clearly than last year, and the year before that, and many years before that.

Another Approach

Under the heading of "If I could do it all over again," I would take another approach to parenting. In spite of the fact that I cannot do it "all" over again, the change of theory is not without immediate value. I have tried to move in another direction during the adolescent years of our children. Simply stated, by taking a more reasonable, enlightened, and celebrative approach to parenting, I might choose to *discover* personality rather than attempt to *shape* it. The first element in such an approach seems best stated as more *responsive* and less *directive*.

I am more aware now than at any other time in my adult life that babies come into the world with a great deal of their personhood already in place. I suspect that parents who assume as much and choose to allow the child to reveal herself/himself will tend to find the parenting task full of surprises and rewards. Who is this new person? Does she prefer to be with people constantly, or does she enjoy being with fewer people? What kinds of food will he enjoy? What kind of order will he choose? Will she enjoy creating or thinking? Will she choose to blend into the world around her, following the lead of others? Will his world be most fulfilling in quiet contemplation or in a whirlwind of activity and sound? How much sleep will he need? Thousands of questions will keep pouring forth as parents try to discover who this child is.

Obviously, developmental tasks play a large part in such discovery: crawling, standing, walking, talking, the development of gross motor skills and fine motor skills, and so on. They all play a part in growth and development; they also tell us a great deal about a child's preferences, inclinations, and disposition. If parents recognize a child as a creature made in the image of God who has brought into the world his or her own uniqueness, the matter of discovery both for the parents and for the child will carry with it a certain reverence. The process will be filled with surprises to which parents can respond, and which will offer no end of influences upon the parents themselves.

I wish I had spent much less time, effort, and energy reading books about parenting, developmental theory, and educational methods; I wish I had given myself to the sheer exuberance of discovery and celebration. I wish I had allowed my children the freedom to explore a great deal more on their own and to take me on their expeditions. I wish I had been more responsive and less directive. Two areas especially call out to me — those involving questions and problem solving.

First, every child indicates some prior direction with each question she asks. I remember one of my fine teachers saying in a classroom setting that we need to allow children to help answer their own questions. (I heard his discussion with an academic mind-set; I was without the experiential wisdom I would later acquire!) My professor suggested we might respond to a child's question by saying, "I know you've thought about that. Tell me what you're thinking." Oh, the confidence a youngster gains from her own explorations when she knows an adult wants to hear her opinion! The answer may be much less important than the process.

Second, every child has some clue to problem solving by the time he demonstrates a need for help or asks for it. "Daddy, help me!" The temptation is always to spare the child the struggle, to solve the problem, to do the job for the child. One man commented rather offhandedly that every hobby he ever took up his father took over. There is a great difference between a minor suggestion to get the child back on track and a complete blueprint.

Educators frequently lament that modern children lack problem-solving skills. Surely part of the reason lies in parents' desires to make life easier for our children, to help them avoid struggles we have faced. Yet, confronting those very struggles and difficulties often allowed us to develop the skills we needed to face greater and greater problems as life became more and more complicated. So it should be for our children.

Television and toys have contributed to our children's paucity of problem-solving and question-answering skills. Much of a child's life seems surrounded, filled, and even cluttered by prepackaged, one-line, or quick-image entertainment. Parents may have difficulty discovering who their child is because the child may be engulfed in an artificial world from early morning until bedtime. The task of self-discovery for a child may be complicated by the brightly colored shapes of plastic toys and the electronic images of video games and television. Such images inundate the mind and overwhelm the emotions.

An empty box or crayons and newsprint may prove to be more thrilling to a child than all the video games in the world. Since they require active engagement and creativity, they will certainly contribute more to the skills of question answering and problem solving. Open-ended activities tend to open lines of communication between parents and the child. While such creative activities contribute to the child's development, they also allow the parents to maintain the process of discovering who the child is and to celebrate that identity.

Does such an approach diminish the importance of parenting, allow parents to abdicate responsibility for the child? Hardly. In fact, parents will discover that when they are needed, they will be needed at much more intense levels. The child who tries and fails will need undivided attention, comfort, and assistance to interpret his failure. At such times, parents may think that it would have been much simpler to have answered the question or solved the problem for the child. We do not want questions and problems to break our children's spirits or overwhelm them; we would, however, like the challenges to strengthen them. Yet if we resist the temptation to direct the learning process involved in these challenges and watch carefully instead, we discover who these children are, and, in some cases, who we are as well.

The second element in a more responsive approach to parenting would surely be a more relaxed and less intense relationship with our children. This flows naturally from the parenting mind-set that chooses to discover rather than to shape and mold. For example, parents who set out to create, mold, and shape a child will tend to be more controlling and rigid and much less flexible than parents who set out on the parental road with a spirit of openness and a desire for discovery. On the one hand, parenting always carries with it some specific goals for the child, rules for the household, and expectations for everyone in the family. On the other hand, parents who set out to discover who the child is and celebrate that identity will naturally approach parenting not so much as a task or a project and more as a journey, a pilgrimage. Instead of "knowing" everything up-front, these parents will share in the learning process with the child. Experience will tend to be more gifted and grace-ful and less an item on a checklist.

None of this is meant to promote passive parenting. We have all seen what happens to children whose parents are physically or emotionally absent from their lives. Discovery is hardly passive. Every sensory nerve-ending and mental capacity may be involved — but does not have to be. We invest as much of ourselves in discovery as we are able. But we do not absent ourselves from watching, listening, and sharing. On occasion we intervene for the child's safety or to protect the child from undertaking certain tasks too soon. Obviously, we would not sit idly by while a toddler steps into the deep end of a swimming pool. Within a few years, however, we may watch proudly as the same child dives into that same depth.

Freedom from constant intensity and a more relaxed and accepting environment communicate stability and security to the child. Such a setting for parenting and growing up communicates trust and engenders confidence in every member of the family. I look back over my years of parenting and realize that many of the things I chose to worry about, deal with, and guide my children toward or away from were probably not worth the emotional energy I invested in them. For example, my wife and I agreed that our children should not use pacifiers, and we discouraged thumb-sucking. In response, they both chose little pillows to carry with them constantly! Over the years we retraced many miles, once returning to a home we had just visited, to recover the pillow one of the girls could not go to bed without. So much for our attempts at shaping and molding.

Another element in the "discover rather than shape" approach to parenting has to do with an increased sense of enjoyment and a reduced burden of obligation. Stated another way, in retrospect I would trade the shoulds, oughts, and musts for more play and celebration. I recognize from this distance that presuppositions tend to dictate both our approaches to parenting and the emotions that attend much of the parenting process. On the one hand, those who seek to create, mold, and shape a new person will tend to be more duty-bound, intense, rigid, and demanding of themselves and everyone around them. On the other hand, those who open themselves to discovery, giftedness, grace, and surprise will tend to be more relaxed, less controlling, and more playful and celebrative.

I return often in my imagination to my own childhood and remember my place in the birth order, my economic milieu, and the determination I either brought into the world or felt imposed upon me by necessity. My own childhood was marked more by demand and duty than by play and celebration. The sense of who I was and how I saw life that I had developed in childhood I carried with me into adulthood and into the "task" of parenting. Had I entered the world of parenting with the mind-set that this was the world of a child who was born a person with some ready-made characteristics, I would surely have approached parenting less as a task. The sense of responsibility would have been softened by the joys of discovery.

Most parents who look back through their years with children recall some potentially happy events they allowed to fade prematurely. How often we hurried away from piano recital or ball game instead of standing around in celebration of the moment and the hard work that preceded the accomplishment! How often we hurried to clean up the mess from the birthday party or the sleep-over only to miss the opportunity to sit amid the clutter and be glad for the laughter and the friends! How often we picked up our child at camp and paid more attention to loading the car than to hearing the stories! As parents we can discover more about our children and ourselves in all the rubble and aftermath of such fun times than we ever discover in preparing for them.

The fourth element of this approach to parenting has to do with an increase in humor and a decline in stifling seriousness. Those of us who have chosen to create, shape, and mold these new persons have taken upon ourselves godlike responsibilities. If the total weight of the "end product" is upon our shoulders, we not only have a difficult time discovering, relaxing, and celebrating; we also find it nearly impossible to laugh at ourselves. Mistakes that we interpret as disasters — whether or not they are! — only increase the pressure, stress, and even fear of ultimate failure.

Humor is not only "God's hand on the shoulder of the troubled world"; it is also an affirmation of faith. Humor acknowledges the importance of human effort, the effort of one human being, but it does not allow that one human being to become supremely important. What our children become — and I'm not always sure what we mean by that! — depends only in part upon what we as parents do. What we are must also be taken into account. More importantly, what the child brings with him or her, the influence of other caring people, and the mysterious presence of God all suggest that parents are not alone in the process. I will say more about these significant others in Chapter Three.

When parents take the path of discovery, becoming responsive to the child, celebrating both the process and the events in the process of growing up, we find more and more occasions for smiles and laughter. How often in retrospect we laugh at what may have disturbed us at the time. Our family now laughs at the memory of Jessica at eighteen months sitting in the middle of shoes in the closet, completely covered with talcum powder, holding the empty can. It was not funny early that Sunday morning! But it is to everyone who has since heard about it. How natural a thing for an inquisitive and playful little one to do! But her serious mother administered a spanking and a tongue-lashing.

Intense, goal-oriented, aggressive, and duty-bound parents seldom laugh. Unfortunate! Children mimic, act out, editorialize, and reflect much of the self-importance and pretense of their serious elders. If we study their artwork, watch them at play, or listen to their interpretations of events, we will discover how funny we are to them. We might also discover how frightening and threatening we are to them. In a very real/surreal sense, children reflect their parents. The more mature we are, the more aware we are of the humor in our lives and in ourselves. The discovery approach to parenting promotes healthy laughter.

Is there no place, then, for shaping, molding, and directing in the lives of our children? Of course there is. The issue is more one of degree than of kind. Do we not all know an athlete whose skills can be attributed in part to her father's interests and abilities in sports? Is it an accident that a great pianist comes from a very musical family? The converse may also be true: the parent who is a successful businessperson may push so hard for the daughter to take over the company that she rejects the world of commerce.

Parents must influence, guide, and protect their children. How we balance these responsibilities with discovery will determine how much relaxed enjoyment we can take in the parenting process and even how much humor we enjoy in the home. Whether our mind-set is that of a creator or that of a pilgrim, we will influence our children. Either way, we will make an imprint on their lives. Our parenting mind-set will in part determine the nature and degree of our influence.

CHAPTER II

What Must This Person Do?

From Beginnings to Four Adolescent Tasks

THE journey from infancy to adulthood, dependence to interdependence, immaturity to maturity takes a long time. Some human beings live to old age without ever quite reaching an effectively functioning adulthood, healthy interdependence, and maturity. Yet, we all have worked and continue to work at the task. Many of the difficulties we have encountered have not been our fault; neither are all the difficulties encountered by our children their fault. We remember from our own childhood and learn from observation that when children are threatened, feel insecure, or face sudden disruptions to an orderly process toward maturity, they let us know. An infant cries when wet or hungry or ill. Similarly, an older child finds a variety of ways to cry out if her world order seems to be coming apart or fails to offer hope and promise. Nightmares, changes in eating or sleeping patterns, feigned illnesses, a change in

35

attitude about school, fighting with other children, a series of broken friendships — all provide clues to parents that something is wrong in the life of their child. Poor academic performance, substance abuse, withdrawal and depression, or other dramatic shifts in behavior patterns tell us that something is wrong in the life of a teenager. Perhaps the most common cause for disruption in a child's orderly progress toward maturity is stress and threat in the home.

Two Signals, Three Causes

My wife and I discovered from our children how change produces cries for help. We moved from one state to another when our girls were seven and twelve years of age. The decision-making process was long and careful; the children were involved the entire time. We believed that they were both dealing with separation from their pleasant, familiar, and orderly world; we were certain that we were interpreting well what lay ahead for them. We listened to what they had to say and tried to discuss every issue they raised.

We were surprised, therefore, when one of our friends told us that Jessica said to her in great seriousness, "A terrible thing has happened to me." When our friend asked Jessica what that was, she responded, "We're moving to Virginia!" My wife and I tried to deal with the "terribleness" of that "thing"; to this day we are not certain we succeeded.

About the time Jessica made the "terrible thing" comment, neighbors who were close friends moved from the community, and she noticed that they put out for trash collection an enormous pile of boxes and throwaway items. She must have thought about that pile of boxes for several days. Finally, she blurted out three questions, almost without punctuation: "Will the people think we don't love them anymore? Will the movers scratch our furniture? Will we have to put out all those boxes?" My wife and I saw immediately that she was addressing the three central issues of every uprooting: rejection, pain, and inventory. We tried to deal with these issues, but we would discover later that we did so unsatisfactorily.

After months of negotiation and planning, I left home in April to assume my new position; the rest of the family stayed behind to complete their school semester. They had the summer to become acclimated to their new home and community. When, in the following fall, Jessica and Portia began their second and sixth year of school respectively, we discovered how unsettled Jessica's world had been. We learned that she had all but stopped work during the second half of first grade; an inattentive teacher had failed to communicate this to us, and we had simply been too occupied with other things to notice it ourselves. Jessica had to do remedial work in the second and third grades, and she might have gotten further behind except for a wise fourth-grade teacher who set her on the catch-up road. Nevertheless, for two years she struggled unhappily with the "terrible thing that had happened to her." That part of her road to maturity and adulthood proved extremely difficult for her.

Jessica had signaled her insecurities through her comments — direct and indirect — and through her schoolwork. For nearly every child, the greater the threat or stress, the more severe the signals. The most obvious causes of the signals are those specific stressors disrupting the orderly world of the child; the deeper causes have much to do with the disruptions in the orderly movement toward maturity, interdependence, and adulthood.

Portia handled the move admirably; her period of stress and distress came later and gradually, with the onset of adolescence. The signals were a sharp drop in academic performance, a gradual withdrawal and depression, and a series of challenges to household rules. On the surface, we interpreted the signals from her as part of the normal process of growing up and the onset of adolescence. We did not see so clearly the larger issue of her struggle toward maturity, adulthood, and interdependence.

The signals from both our children gradually became clearer. We began to realize the degree to which they felt the stress of the transition from one community to another and from one stage of development to the next. There was also a third factor their parents could not/would not see until the signals became more dramatic: our own relationship had reached a period of transition. My wife had chosen to return to graduate school as part of a career change. The process of her decision had raised questions about how she and I made decisions, related to one another, and functioned as parents. At forty-plus years of age, we were discovering that some of the work necessary for our own maturity and interdependence had not been completed. Our struggle and tension because of these critical deficiencies in our own lives were creating dis-ease and threats for our children. We now know that even when families do not function well, but function consistently, children may follow predictable and even acceptable patterns of behavior. When the rules of family function are changed, however, stress often occurs, and the children act out their own insecurities. None of us cares a great deal for change. Parents care even less for those severely acted out signals from their children.

Nevertheless, in our family the natural tensions of childhood development and the added strain of a re-negotiated marriage contract proved to be growth-inducing, soul-stirring, and strengthening for each of us as individuals and for our family unit. The process lasted nearly a decade, and in some ways it continues. I cannot say at what point I came to understand analytically what was happening, but some clarity gradually began to emerge. What I saw transcended our family situation; I discerned more clearly four adolescent tasks common to every person in our culture. These requirements for adulthood, maturity, and interdependence tend to be understated but important in early childhood, more evident and vital in later childhood, and absolutely essential during adolescence. My own experiences as a father forced me to ask serious questions not only about our methods of parenting but also about the very goals and needs of all human beings on their way to adulthood. Part of my own questioning led me to look at the kinds of qualities all of us need if we are to function as mature adults. I came to understand that I myself, in middle age, had unfinished business at this point. I realized that the future of my children depended upon how well they approached some specific tasks of growing up. Those tasks, I came to realize, are concerned with identity, power, authority, and intimacy.

The Adolescent Tasks:
Before, During, and After the Teen Years

Four issues in the process of growing up seem to loom largest during adolescence. This period when so much is changing in a person's life and when responsibilities seem greater and greater often becomes the most stormy and stressful. Parents can deal better with the intensity of this developmental period if we have, among other tools and skills, some basic understanding of these adolescent tasks. If we think through our own progress or lack of it during our own adolescence, we will be more sympathetic toward the struggles of our children.

The first of these issues/tasks is IDENTITY — who am I? We ask the child, "Whose little girl are you?" or "Whose little boy are you?" The answer we want is that the child belongs to mommy or daddy. We begin to teach a child very early about identity — using the child's name frequently, explaining to whom the child belongs. We often use mirrors and photography as part of playful and affectionate who-are-you games to send the message that the child is important to parents, extended family and friends, and God. The child is hardly aware that he is developing a sense of person-hood, but these things help create a sense of self-worth — and sometimes an unfortunate sense of ownership.

Self-esteem is influenced early but never written in stone. A major crisis can shake even the most self-confident person at any point in life; the more fragile ego of a child is vulnerable even to minor crises. The security of home and family allow the child a safe place to sort out crises and threats from the outside world and to emerge even more self-confident. But when those threats occur within the family — in the form of abuse, criticism, ridicule, unreasonable expectations, and/or violence — the child's self-esteem may hit rock bottom, and she may recover only with years of psychotherapy. The issue is identity: Who am I?

Even when childhood is normal, happy, and re-warding, something begins to happen to that emerging identity when the child reaches puberty. The body changes. The beautiful complexion may become pimply. The petite little girl may gain weight. The very normal-looking little boy may grow by leaps and bounds and become what seems to him to be abnor-mally skinny. His voice changes. She begins menses.

41

Someone suggested that teenagers spend increasing amounts of time in front of mirrors because they need to see if they are still there!

Where did the person he once was go? Who is this in the mirror in front of her? Any failure or criticism takes on the proportions of a crisis. Competition with other youngsters seems to be everywhere, even when it doesn't exist. Friendships are often delicate and shifting. Mood swings occur almost instantaneously. A young person may insist that she is "different" but dress like a clone of other young people who also believe they are different. Identity seems terribly bound up with the group because whoever these young people were in childhood no longer seems to be relevant. Most children experience a significant drop in self-confidence at the beginning of adolescence. The who-am-I question looms larger and larger.

One of the more delicate issues the parent faces in this struggle has to do with expectations. If the parent functions as the creator, shaper, and molder of the child, this period of struggle with self-esteem raises all manner of questions about the quality of the parent's craft. "If my child is not sure of himself, excelling in school, or behaving like a mature adult (since he now has the grown-up body of an adult!), I must have failed." In desperation, the parent may press the youngster with higher and higher goals and expectations. Every lapse, every mood swing, every uncertainty on the part of the teenager may be seen like a negative reflection upon the godlike parent.

If, on the other hand, the parent shares in the young person's pilgrimage, watching and encouraging the emergence of this person, the parent will offer a calm and affirming anchor. I recall many dinnertime discussions in which Portia complained that she could not attain what my wife and I expected of her. We denied her charges (rather than discuss them specifically and in detail!), and countered with the defense that parents expect a great deal only because they love their children. She was alert enough to know we loved her; she also knew that parents often expect a great deal from children because parents love themselves and want to look good through their children. She was correct, and for a long time we had difficulty accepting her critique.

Parents who can affirm and encourage their teenagers during these years of struggle with identity will contribute far more this way than by forcing their own goals on their children. This is not to say that we should have no expectations or rules; the point is that we should discuss and renegotiate our dreams for our children throughout their childhood. By the time adolescence begins, the young person should clearly discern two anchors: first, the stability, love, and encouragement of the parents, and second, a sense of who he or she is in the eyes of God. Parents who are capable of humor and who tend to be more responsive than directive, more relaxed than intense, and more celebrative than obligated tend to provide an atmosphere of calm during the period of the teenager's uncertainty.

That second anchor, too seldom discussed in association with a young person's struggle with identity, is a transcendent issue: Who does God think this teenager is? The biblical witness about our identity as persons is unmistakable. At the beginning and the end of holy scripture we are told that we are made in the image of God (Gen. 1:26) and that we are God's children, brought into God's family by the power of love (1 John 3:1). When parents express the biblical witness to their children through their words and attitudes, and when they reiterate that message to teenagers in their struggles with identity, children have a strong foundation on which to build their identity.

The struggle with identity begins in early childhood, intensifies during adolescence, and continues into early adulthood. Perhaps we should say that parents help children identify what makes them unique as persons in their own eyes, in their parents' eyes, and in God's eyes. Parents can also help their children understand that all of us experience self-doubts and transitions, even failures, all of which can strengthen us — even when we are grown-up. This sense of self provides the foundation for the other tasks of adolescence.

The second of these adolescent tasks or struggles has to do with AUTHORITY. Who makes the rules in a person's life? Before whom do we live our lives? To whom are we accountable and at what level?

The life of Jesus is instructive at this point. When he was twelve years old, he became separated from his parents in Jerusalem. When they reprimanded him, he answered them by indicating his awareness of another Parent (Luke 2:49). Yet, the evangelist tells us that Jesus returned home with them and lived under their authority (Luke 2:51). Later in life, in his early adulthood, he was told that his mother and brothers were asking to see him. His response? His real kin were those who heard God's message and put it into practice (Luke 8:19-21). Jesus was hardly rejecting his family; he was stating clearly his higher authority.

Bishop James Pike of the Episcopal Church is reported to have said, "No one has authority who does not first stand under authority." The authority of experience, longevity, and adulthood must be bought and paid for with a healthy submission to other authorities as we grow up. If a society is to avoid anarchy and maintain order, some workable chain of authority must be established; the same may be said of every institution, including the family.

The first authority a child encounters is that of parents. The circle — or hierarchy — expands to include relatives, friends, and teachers. In some sense, these forms of authority hold sway because they are benevolent, administered lovingly and for the good of the child. The child may test the limits of this authority, but because of his or her relative size and powerlessness, and because of the benevolence attached to such order, the child will not engage in serious rebellion. Nevertheless, human freedom of will and a desire to test the boundaries always lead to some family conflicts; children will test their parents, if for no other reason than to discover how hard they can push. I remember one of my favorite professors making such a point: "Why did the kids put beans in their ears when the last thing we told the kids was not to put beans in their ears! Why did the kids put molasses on the cat when the last thing we told the kids was not to put molasses on the cat!"

Adolescence seems to be the period of the most severe testing of limits. These "children" have attained a physical size and maturity that makes them feel some parity with adults, and they have also gained enough freedom to explore the outer boundaries of their world. Parents do well to separate rebellion against their authority from the healthy and normal testing of boundaries. I have often noticed pastures for cattle, carefully fenced. Along every fence is a well-worn path, created by the animals testing the limits, looking for open places or a weak spot in the fence. To use another image that links authority with identity, parents are the anvils — the central authority — on which young people hammer out their identities. The testing is not always against parents, not always personal; to interpret all testing as defiance against parents tends to raise the normal process to crisis levels.

How well I remember Portia's outlandish costumes purchased at used-clothing stores, the music that never seemed like music to me, the posters of strange-looking and seductive music and movie personalities. I feel some sadness that I was not able to face these symbolic tests of the boundaries with more humor, with a more relaxed and less intense spirit. But I recall just as vividly how clothing selection later took a more conservative direction, even including an occasional dress and heels. I remember the day the bizarre posters were replaced with new ones bearing poetry, proverbs, and other words of wisdom. I recall the evolution of musical taste, when the "headbanging" variety was replaced with the more thoughtful and less strident variety, and an occasional piece from the classical repertoire.

What many parents fear — and suffer through — are the rebellions that go far beyond the normal testing of authority: substance abuse, driving violations, shoplifting, vandalism, fighting, and promiscuity. In the normal process of testing authority, some acceptance of authority remains; in rebelliousness, all authority tends to be rejected. Parents do well to sort out the difference and avoid treating one as the other.

Ultimately, all mature, responsible, and interdependent adults must come out on the side of accepting various kinds and levels of authority. Teenagers do learn that all authority can be questioned and that rules may be negotiated. They must also learn how to do both to their own advantage and within acceptable boundaries. Parents can open the doors to such questions and challenges very early. I recall an inspiring conference with a teacher. One of our girls came home from school one day terribly upset because the entire class had been chastised for something one student had done. We talked about it, and I offered to go with her to talk with the teacher. Although she felt some trepidation, she agreed to do so. She told the teacher what she disagreed with, and as I expected, the teacher heard her and admitted that teachers make mistakes too. She apologized to my daughter, and to the class the next day. In this way children can learn the flexibility of authority — but they will still need to test it.

Adolescents should be encouraged to confer with teachers, attend government meetings, and write letters to newspaper editors and politicians. The greater the number of appropriate means of testing authority that young people have available to them, the fewer inappropriate challenges to authority they are likely to attempt. However, parents should not expect no challenge to authority at all; that in itself would be cause for concern.

Identity and self-esteem are enhanced when we recognize that we are made in the image of God and are loved into being as children of God; in the same way, authority will become a safe and secure aspect of life when we reach an awareness that each person who has authority must also stand under authority. As adolescents move in this direction, they are moving toward adulthood, maturity, and interdependence.

The third task of adolescents is learning to deal with and use POWER. The progress from nearly complete helplessness at birth to some measure of self-sufficiency/interdependence requires careful guidance by parents and society. Children soon learn about power. They can cry and scream as a means of controlling or manipulating an entire household. Ask any mother who has walked the floor with a crying child;

the child has the power, intended or not, to control the parent. Think about the little one in a high chair who learned how quickly everyone in the family jumped when he pushed his feet against the table and began to tip over backwards!

Little by little, children learn what "hooks," "pulls the chain," or "touches a nerve" in various adults. By the time a youngster is sixteen, he or she has an enormous arsenal or set of tools — depending upon his or her relative maturity — available or in place. The most significant of these are a driver's license, a job, and sexual capacities. While such means of power are accessible and have great potential for good, they can also be used to harm and even destroy health, happiness, and life itself.

In the eyes of nearly all young people, the most important possession is a driver's license. This little card symbolizes a giant step toward independence. As one of our girls kept saying, "I'll be glad when I don't have to depend on somebody else every time I need to go someplace!" Wheels mean a new level of freedom. Walking enabled the child to explore a short distance from parents; a bike extended the distance beyond the watchful eyes of mom and dad; a car opens what seems like the whole world.

That driver's license becomes a powerful tool, liberating both the young person and also the taxi-driver parent. What is more often verbalized, however, is the potential the car has as a weapon. Underdeveloped driving skills, a youthful sense of invulnerability, a need to show off, a lack of concentration — all transform a wonderful tool into a potential weapon of disaster. Does the time ever come when a parent falls into calm sleep before a teenage driver comes home? I think not. Enormous power!

Money also represents power. Almost as soon as a child learns to count, what is counted most is money. Children learn early that coins, bills, checks, and credit cards can be used to purchase whatever they want. If we say, "I don't have any money for that!" the children reply, "Just write a check!" I no longer remember at what early age our children began to ask for toys, clothing, and shoes by brand names. These status symbols were themselves the power of acceptance or dominance in peer groups; the power behind the power was always the money to purchase the status symbols.

Year by year the stakes grow as the symbols cost more and more. Teenagers become as frustrated in the struggle to have it all as they are in depending upon others to transport them. I watched as our children manipulated allowance and extra money earned through odd jobs; I watched as the baby-sitting money created a larger pool of purchasing power; I watched when baby-sitting was traded for part-time jobs with hourly wages and sizeable paychecks. At one point I realized my children had more unobligated and spendable money each week than I had. All along the way we negotiated on setting aside a percentage for church/charitable gifts and savings and designating the remaining amount as discretionary funds.

With such power comes tension. Parents see their teenagers preferring to work rather than acccompany the family on vacations or spend holidays at home. A part-time job may replace extracurricular activities at school. Work may interfere with church attendance and compete with schoolwork, leisure reading, and play. Young people seek to exercise their earning power, and parents try to direct it toward benefit and away from harm. The middle ground usually proves to be a wavy line!

The third aspect of power in the life of the teenager is sex. This, perhaps, is the most powerful tool and the one most feared by parents. These young bodies, fully developed and surging with desire, are at the mercy of immature minds and emotions. Pregnancy, disease, and emotional trauma seem lame reasons for sexual abstinence in a world where nothing is more important than the rights and wishes of the individual, and this is especially true for teenagers, whose power is so newly acquired. Statistics about teenage sexual activity, pregnancy, and disease are astounding and frightening.

Parents who choose to respond rather than shape, to take a more relaxed and celebrative approach to their task, will be severely tested during this period of their youngsters' lives. The responsive parent, however, will travel somewhere between the completely permissive way and the way of inflexibility and rigidity. Parents who take the responsive, relaxed, and humor-tinged approach from the time their child is born will bear a far less heavy burden during the child's teen years than will parents who believe that everything the child becomes depends totally on mom and dad.

After more than two decades of parenting and a shift of approaches midstream, I am able to admit to myself that I cannot go everywhere my girls go, watch every move they make, drive the cars for them, choose their friends, manage their money, or make their sexual decisions for them. Bit by bit they have accumulated enormous power to decide where they go, power to get money and spend it, and power to decide how they will use their sexual capabilities, including the capability to create new life or even to destroy their own lives. I have been able to discuss in detail my role as their father; they may choose how to use their power, and I am free to choose how I will respond if they misuse that power. Neither of us may agree completely with the other; neither of us has absolute power over the other in decision making or responses. We are all growing in our understanding of our individual power and the power of our relationships.

The final "adolescent task" is developing INTIMACY. This is related to each of the other three, but it is the most difficult to develop — or perhaps we should say the easiest to damage. I suspect all human beings are born with the gift of closeness. That early bonding between mother and infant creates the openness to the possibility of closeness with other human beings. As the infant grows, he or she must learn to differentiate among many kinds, expressions, and levels of intimacy. The positive development, however, is much easier than the repair of damage done by insensitivity, smothering, rejection, or abuse.

I remember well a stray dog that came to our farm when I was a boy. He was hungry — for food and affection. When he saw any of us, however, he cowered and retreated with his tail tucked between his legs. He had probably been cared for by his mother, open to affection from other creatures, until some person mistreated him and taught him to withdraw. So with most human beings. Harsh words, inappropriate criticism, silent disapproval, and physical abuse or neglect have driven wedges and erected barriers between people; to the mistreated individual, every other human being may become suspect, a potential enemy, a threat.

Most adults can recall as vividly as if it had happened yesterday some incident of being laughed at by classmates, harshly criticized by a teacher, or betrayed by a friend. A parent may complain that his child never talks to him; the child may have tried without success to get through the newspaper or a televised ballgame. Once the damage is done, intimacy with every other human being has been made more difficult. We have all heard someone in pain vow, "Nobody will ever hurt me again!" Yet, intimacy implies vulnerability and risk; interpreting and learning from failure is part of growth toward the more mature levels of closeness.

Even parents who desperately wish to do everything right and be the best they can be may damage

53

the closeness they have enjoyed early on with their children. I live with the memory of the many times I have shifted too quickly into the teaching/helping/interpreting mode rather than celebrate whatever was accomplished while the glow was still warm. My effort to help very often seemed like criticism of the child and rejection of the effort. "That's nice, but. . . ." I heard my words replayed in the protests of my children about expectations. Instead of responding, I took it upon myself to set goals I had no right to set. The expectations created a standard for criticism, rejection, and distance. Repairing such damage requires more effort and time than it took to inflict it.

If this level of damage to closeness runs deep, imagine what harm direct, harsh, demeaning statements inflict. Even more severe are all forms of physical abuse. With so much damage done to children as they grow up, should we be surprised that teenagers struggle to find appropriate means to develop and communicate closeness with other young people? Sometimes the very adults who have damaged the teenager's ability to express intimacy appropriately are those who try to help the youngster when problems with intimacy occur with other young people.

Adults who have taken a more flexible, responsive approach to parenting find that intimacy tends to develop with less damage between themselves and their children. In a more relaxed environment, humor and playfulness allow for a freer expression of feelings. On the other hand, an atmosphere of constant seriousness, intensity, and unbendingly high expectations fosters distance, loneliness, and fear of failure. The pressure may at times produce arguments, accusations, and threats. The damage done is long-term: teenagers inevitably carry the same responses and reactions into relationships that they develop with those outside their families, and the pattern may be lifelong.

Never Too Late

In a very real sense, all of us struggle with who we are, to whom we answer, the amount and kinds of power we possess, and how to live in relative closeness with the people who mean most to us. We need to make major progress in all these areas, however, before we can consider ourselves mature, responsible, and interdependent human beings. The forty-year-old person whose life is pocked by sexual promiscuity has made little progress in that adolescent task. A fifty-year-old businessperson who bullies everyone still faces the adolescent task of learning to use power and accept appropriate authority. Many, if not most, of the problems adults have with money management, authority, self-image, sexual function, and commitment can be traced to tasks long since deserted, tasks that should have been progressing well by early adulthood.

The good news, however, is that every signal of dysfunction, whenever it occurs, can call us to account. We can take up the unfinished adolescent task and rejoin the pilgrimage we thought we had completed. What may be the most surprising aspect of parenting becomes the role reversal, or at least the equalizing process. The child becomes the parent in the best sense of the word — teaching, helping, supporting and encouraging, participating in the work at hand. At the very least the parent joins the child/adolescent in the growing process. Failure and/or dysfunction remind us that we too are human, that we are not the Creator, the ultimate authority or absolute power.

What must this child do? This child must do the work of becoming a mature, responsible, and interdependent adult. And so must his or her parents.

CHAPTER III

Adolescent Storms: Not All Bad News

FOR many years our refrigerator bore beneath a small magnet a newspaper cartoon that finally wore out from being bumped around and shared with friends. An elementary school teacher is shown reading a note that had been pinned to a small girl's dress, the note obviously from an embarrassed but defeated mother: "I hope you don't think I picked out this outfit!" That scenario provides chapter, verse, and commentary on my assessment of the kind of job I did as a parent. The cartoon says volumes about the tension between the expectations of parents and the personalities, wishes, and revolts of children. The laughter from a cartoon diverts us as parents from the importance we tend to place upon looking good or at least not looking bad to the outside world, especially through our children.

If any period in my children's growing-up process revealed my own not-so-subtle expectations and their less-than-subtle rejection of those expectations, it was their puberty and adolescence. (The signs were everywhere much earlier; I chose to ignore them!) But then, isn't that when it usually occurs! I still recall those rapier-like thrusts that came in our family conversations at dinnertime: "I can't live up to your expectations!"

And I responded, "Would you prefer that I have no expectations? Can't you see that whatever expectations we [Notice, when trapped I always sought alliance with my wife!] have are part of our love for you and concern for your well-being?"

She didn't buy it. "What you care about is how you look to other people."

Who says teenagers can't think straight?

"I hope you don't think I picked out this outfit!" The cartoon sounds a little distant thunder from as far away as childhood. The storms would find their way overhead much later. And when it rains, it often pours.

The View from the Middle of the Storm

The year a child is fifteen is a difficult time of life. Those agonizing months were certainly difficult for our family — not once but twice. Most youngsters experience the storms when they are about sixteen or seventeen. On average, the most difficult years seem to be from age fifteen through age seventeen. As difficult as these years may be for both parents and children, what seems so traumatic may not in fact be so bad. When parents want to be perfect, however, any flaw or trouble spot tends to become cataclysmic.

First came the music. Of course, my wife and I knew the girls wouldn't always sit in that pile of children's records and soundtracks from *Mary Poppins* and *The Sound of Music*. But we were hardly prepared for the substitute. I was much less engrossed in rock music when I was a teenager, so I had no idea what was to come. Our daughters' earliest ventures into music of the younger generation were relatively tame, even though we suspected that the elephant wanted his trunk in the tent not so much to get it warm, but to take over the entire tent. But we watched the progression from the young, all-American, guitar-playing, fun-loving hero to those characters who looked and sounded as though they spent most of their time in underground solitary confinement. Their music was often strident and grating, hostile and rebellious. Their appearance said very quickly that they chose not to be a part of the mainstream society I lived in and preferred for my children. I disliked the music and the suggestive posters that took over the rooms with white dressers and lacy curtains. It all seemed so incongruent.

What should perfect parents do about this invasion? To prohibit all such teenage interests would certainly be counterproductive. After all, my wife and I reasoned, if we had done our job well to this point, the religious training, the cultural influences, and the standards and values we had shared with our children would outweigh what seemed in theory so foreign yet now so real a part of our lives. We negotiated our daughters' acquisition of records and posters, the amount of time they spent watching television and listening to rock music, and even the purchase for each of them of a stereo system better than the one I owned. We arrived at some compromise about the volume of the music. In short, we handled as best we could what we as parents disliked. To this day, however, we believe the influence of much of that music and those musical groups has been detrimental. Yet, we remain pleased that our daughters' choices from among all the kinds of rock music available were comparatively well-made. Neither girl chose what would be considered the extreme end of the rock spectrum. That notwithstanding, what they did choose was nothing like what I would have chosen for them if I could have done so. But to have forced my preferences upon our daughters would have proven unwise.

Another area of conflict and tension had to do with those outfits that I did not choose. Portia took to the used-clothing stores. In fact, I recall now with some humor and a little chagrin a trip to New York City. It was a birthday gift to mark all the exciting aspects of turning sixteen! Our daughter wanted to do two things: she wanted to see some Broadway plays — which we were pleased to arrange — and she wanted to shop in some strange, used-clothing stores. For one entire day we trekked the streets of Greenwich Village and Soho, looking through some of the most outlandish places and most incredible clothes I have ever seen. And we brought home some of those garments.

Again, what are perfect parents to do? Just say No? Enjoy the humor of 365 days of Halloween? I remembered my own high school years of ducktails, blue jeans worn without a belt and low on the hips, white T-shirts with the sleeves rolled up or cut off. How long could it last? A couple of years or so, and what harm could it do? Again, we acquiesced in order to avoid some conflict, choosing carefully which battles we would fight. (Incidentally, the "battle" image would soon come into play.) Portia, who seemed to have no interest in playing "dress-up" as a child, plunged into it with a vengeance as a teenager; Jessica, who all through childhood owned a trunk of dress-up costumes, carried her interests right on into her late teen years. Hers, however, was a much less dramatic performance than that of her older sister. We didn't mind a bit.

Perhaps one added dimension of rock music and adolescent costuming was pierced ears. Portia had three holes in one ear; seven in the other! That's right, seven! She wore a loop in the bottom hole and the six letters of her name — or other collections of earrings — in the other six places. If attention was the object, she got it — everywhere. Did it hurt? Who did you get to do it for you? What do your parents think of that? Now that we look back on it, it seemed to fit the clothing and the music and the posters in her room. Whoever her parents were and whatever they had hoped for her were being cast aside.

This was also the period in which we saw her grades drop from A's and B's to B's and C's and an occasional D. We also saw the most frightening dimension of all — depression and talk of suicide. As far as we ever knew, she used no drugs and very little alcohol. A series of violations of major household rules coupled with talk of death and suicide finally made my wife and me recognize our need for help — for us as a family rather than for Portia alone.

We recognized that the things we were going through were probably quite similar to the agonies of many if not most families with teenagers. We saw in our circle of friends, our church, our school, and our neighborhood all the manifestations of struggle in the lives of these young people. We saw extensive drug use, alcohol consumption of epidemic proportions, sexual promiscuity with all the attendant consequences, suicide, runaways, violations of the law, and explosive relationships between parents and teenagers. My work as a member of the clergy brought me into steady contact with families in the midst of such stress and with teenagers in need of help. My contacts with the mental health profession made me keenly aware of the extent and degree of the turbulence of these years. In my own arrogance and overconfidence, I had been certain that such explosions would never occur in my family; my children would handle adolescence as if they were adults. Oh, the difference between theory and practice! Yet, for all the theory and practice, our daughters probably experienced a much less stormy period than many young people do. A significant number of their struggles proved to be necessary or the result of issues not of their own choosing. Nevertheless, my unrealistic expectations made those experiences more agonizing for me than any other experiences in my entire life.

Some Analysis

The journey from infancy to adulthood, dependence to interdependence, immaturity to maturity intensifies at puberty — about twelve years of age or so — and turns dramatically uphill in midadolescence — fifteen to seventeen years of age. For some young people, the climb extends far into the twenties. On the one hand, my wife and I witnessed the struggles of our teenagers to become adults, drive a car, earn money, try to manage authority and sexuality. We watched as our daughters explored and experimented with decision making and conflict management with their parents and friends. We listened to them philosophize about the world around them. On the other hand, and sometimes in the same day, hour, or breath, we noticed their retreat to stuffed animals, dolls, and Sesame Street. Portia, now in young adulthood, still enjoys occasionally her collection of Bugs Bunny videotapes and a box of sixty-four crayons. In adolescents the desire to be adults and the fear of adulthood clash day by day, and for a long time.

Part of the tension comes from those bodies almost

fully developed, complete with sexual desire, and those minds and emotions still more tied to childhood. Additional pressures come from expectations from the adult world and pressure from the media and from peers. Adults tell them constantly to be careful; their peers call to them to take risks. Adults push them to study hard so that they will score well on college boards, get into a good college, and get a good job; their peers tell them about the fun that awaits them in the world beyond high school. Adults beg them to save their money for a rainy day; their peers tell them it is raining now.

After years of such struggle and tension in my family's life, we now enjoy hearing the accounts of our daughters' memories of childhood and early adolescence. Apparently, a significant turning point for Portia was the day we sat down and determined that there should be some specified household chores. As she recalls it, that was the day she went from a carefree child to a person with important responsibilities. We obviously handled that transition poorly, failing to connect the clean-up/pick-up, dishwashing, and laundry folding of her early childhood with the more clearly specified work in her later childhood. Much of what we hear now reinforces what we have learned about the difficult and painful transition from childhood to adulthood.

If parents very early speculate "Who is this person?" the adolescent asks almost feverishly, "Who am I?" Both parents and peers are mirrors of the different manifestations of that shifting identity. Teenagers may see their parents as humorless, overworked, worried, and devoid of fun; they may see their friends, whom they envy and emulate at the same time, as shallow, irresponsible, and out of control. They can be critical of both, almost in the same sentence. On the one hand, they look forward to being away from home and on their own; on the other hand, they suffer from self-doubts about their ability to make it on their own.

In many cases, parents find themselves confused about their youngsters. At the very time of life when adolescents want and need a listener, an adult to hug them and reassure them, parents misinterpret the clothing and the loud music and the language of rebellion to mean the opposite. Very often parents have invested enormous energy in the childhood years only to discover that the real energy is needed in the teen years; by that time, they are too tired. In many cases parents dislike their teenagers or feel inadequate to meet the needs of their teenagers; therefore, they retreat into silence or busyness or other forms of avoidance. Both young people and parents become locked in games of concern and retreat, care and judgment, need and rejection. Such is the common pattern of normal adolescent transition. Perhaps it is all nature's way of preparing parent and young person for that inevitable and healthy separation only a few years away.

Yet, another not-so-normal and frequently denied aspect of adolescent turmoil is an attempt to correct what may be wrong with the way a family functions.

The stormy behavior of many teenagers occurs because some things are very wrong with their family systems. As long as they are children, relatively powerless and not very analytical, they may know something is wrong at home but accept it because they have no choice or have little with which to compare their situations. By early adolescence, when they have gained more power and have more information with which to assess their situations, many young people begin to realize that some functioning of their families is stifling at best and destructive at worst.

Studies of families conflicted by alcoholism, domestic violence, and/or abuse indicate that children and especially adolescents act out in severe ways various protests against wrongs and injustices the entire family experiences. Parents in such homes may seek counseling for their adolescents as the ones with "the problem." Those same parents tend to be reluctant to look at a larger and more adult-centered problem. As long as the issue is drugs or alcohol or promiscuity or running away from home or problems with the law or dress or hairstyle or poor academic performance, the source of the conflict is the teenager; the parents tend not to accept much if any of the responsibility.

Sorting It All Out

Analysis of the problems and causes tends to run the gamut from difficult to impossible, especially while families are besieged by storms. All my family knew during Portia's struggles during her midteen years (fifteen, sixteen, seventeen) was sadness, vaguely stated wishes, irritating challenges to household rules, and occasional but bitter accusations against "perfect parents." During this period my wife and I began to face the harsh realization that we were renegotiating, somewhat painfully, our marriage contract, and in retrospect, we can see that we resented having to deal with an ungrateful, rebellious teenager. Jessica was caught in the middle of it all — a peacemaker, protector, and reluctant interpreter.

We found the threat to our family to be overwhelming, depressing, and exhausting for each of us in individual ways. We all tried to function as normally as possible in our work and at school, but none of us had much heart for it. We realized in the midst of the wind and hail that our tent was not as well anchored as we the parents had wanted to believe. In response, we sought the counsel of a longtime friend and psychotherapist.

I was knowledgeable enough about the psychotherapeutic process to understand that we were not dealing with an adolescent adjustment problem; ours was a family system malfunction. Our family system operated acceptably until one member of the family found it inadequate and threw herself on the line to break the pattern. We did not fully realize for many months what was happening. We went to see our therapist/friend; we explained, dutifully and professionally, that we had a family problem and that we all wanted to work on it together. We did so for a time, until the therapist chose to see our daughter privately. The major turning point for all of us proved to be terrifying beyond all our imaginations.

One day the counselor called me from the waiting room into his outer office and said to me in anxious tones, "We have to get her into the hospital! She is dangerously suicidal." Lightning had struck the tent! That thirty-day hospitalization proved to be a real crisis of danger and opportunity for our family. We discovered much later that the root cause of the depression was a partial side-effect from a physical problem and prescription medication. Secondarily, but perhaps more importantly, the depression and rebellion were part of a very bright girl's attempt to change the direction of an entire family system that was not functioning in her best interests. In many ways, hers was a heroic effort, made at the potential cost of her own life. We continue to discover pieces of the fallout from the explosion. There was no suicide attempt. There was little irreparable damage. There were a number of revelations; some continue to show up in the light of our continuing growth.

One enormously important glimmer of awareness has to do with the excellence of my intention and the mediocrity of my functioning as a parent. Part of my intent to create, mold, and shape personhood — as ill-advised as that was! — included a desire that our children would become independent and confident individuals. In retrospect, I would now hope for them to be interdependent, which is very different from being independent. I would like for them to be confident and individualistic within their larger communities. But I now know I could not program those directions, nor did I do well what I had so ill-advisedly attempted.

In reality, what I wanted for my children I often sabotaged through the way I functioned: I was loving and caring, but overprotecting. I offered instruction and advice far too freely. I intervened to help far too frequently. I watched and listened much less intently than was good for my daughters. I feared for their well-being and sought to spare them the pain of failure and the exhaustion of effort. Even after several years of learning and re-orienting my role as parent, the old ways and old desires keep pressing upon me.

A case in point. When she was twenty-one, Portia decided to live in her college town during the summer between her third and final years of school. She wanted to take two courses in the summer terms, work part-time, and live in her own apartment. We had agreed as a family that the time was right for such a transition. My wife and I offered to apply room-and-board fees at school to her apartment costs with the understanding that she would cover the remaining expenses with earnings from her part-time work. We offered a few items of furniture and our help when she moved in. When the time came and the apartment and the apartment mates were selected, however, I began to offer objections. Leasing had to be done carefully. Could she afford the additional expense? Could she accept not being able to afford some of the things she had had money to do during the past year? How dependable were the other two young women she would be living with? The apartment was seven miles from campus. Couldn't she find something closer?

She finally reminded me that she functions differently than I do. She is a natural risk-taker. She had chosen a more expensive place because she knew her parents preferred that she live in the safest environment possible. I thought about it and realized that she was right, and that she was also twenty-one years of age. I wrote her a note and told her to go for it! She understood fully the limits of my commitment to the costs and the extent of her responsibilities. My daughter was functioning as an interdependent, confident individualist who would not let me revert to my old protectionist mode of operation.

Yet, the journey to this point has not been easy; the struggle has been constant and always more or less uphill. We as parents may alter the behavior patterns we have formed over a period of several decades in our lives, but never without hard work and consistent challenges by those who care enough to risk the reprisals when we turn them aside. Again comes the Wordsworthian wisdom: "The child is father of the man."

In recent years I have thought many times about how Portia and Jessica have provided me with opportunities to relive my own youth, to discover much of what I missed in my own growing-up years: with them I have been able to enjoy reading children's books, playing children's games, traveling, exploring, and even celebrating. These are gifts I have been given through my children — and what I have learned from their growing up has also been a gift, a lesson worth learning. Just as they have had to struggle to become mature and responsible adults, so I have had to struggle with the realization that the challenges are not over when one reaches adulthood. Parenting teaches us in special ways that we face change and hence risk as long as we live.

In that sense, the storms need not be utterly destructive. Unless mediocrity and misdirection are challenged, they multiply and increase the miles of lostness. In many cases — no, in most cases — the problems children cause in their growing up are legitimate cries for help or protests against something wrong in their family systems. Their parents need not be malicious, incompetent, or even negligent. Rather, as I have been, parents may be too directive, overinvolved, and smothering. Any strength, even caring, can become a weakness if pushed to its extreme.

Jessica has perhaps been both victim and recipient of the benefits of our family's stormy period. I suspect that as Portia took a great risk to change the course of our misdirection, so Jessica bore a silent burden of worry in the midst of instability. Was she to betray her sister during those violations of household rules, even for her sister's own good and even though her sister was really crying out for help? She chose to remain silent, trying to be the perfect child, attempting to compensate for the imperfections in Portia. We are reminded in retrospect how desperately some family members will try to compensate in order to keep the system functioning in ways which have always seemed normal, even if that functioning is counterproductive and unsatisfactory. Most of us prefer the unacceptable known to the potentially better but vague unknown.

Jessica sacrificed much of the fun and carefree playfulness that is usually a part of later childhood through her worrying and overachieving. In her own adolescence she has faced the struggle between work and play, compliance with and healthy challenges to the expectations of others, independence and interdependence. We have no idea how much personal responsibility she feels for the tensions of those years of family turmoil; in all likelihood, she is still only partially in touch with those feelings. Nevertheless, we continue to discover many dimensions of her pain from those years.

One positive aspect of our growth as a family has been a greater degree of freedom for Jessica. I have attempted to be far less directive and far more responsive in my involvement in her choices and decisions. Her mother has been far more available to her, and she has also been far more involved in her decision making processes than she was with Portia, and more involved than I have been in these processes. This has been by design and agreement. We have all learned something about the importance of each parent operating from his or her strengths and backing off in those areas in which he or she tends to revert back to being either overly directive or underinvolved.

We have watched with some pleasure and pride as Jessica has maintained a high level of academic achievement, intentional involvement in church activities, and a busy social life. Her challenges to our system, her protests against certain household rules, and her expressions of individualism have been far less strident and abrasive than they might have been under our former system. We have noticed a much healthier kind of conflict management, decision making, and time management on her part, and on ours.

Of course, we are frequently faced with comparisons. Each issue that proves to involve tension causes her mother and me to recall painful memories and to fear repeated upheaval. "Oh, oh! Here it goes again!" She is cat-like in her quickness to remind us of what she senses. Yet, we know how often she has chosen to avoid many of the shouting matches, tears, threats, and accusations she remembers so well.

Perhaps the greatest benefit of the storms in Portia's adolescence has been the value to my wife and me. In what may be an overstatement, we can say, "We have seen the enemy and he is us!" My wife and I now realize that not only in parenting but in every aspect of our relationship we tended to become "polarized" on most major issues. If I took a firm stand on discipline of the children, homework, curfews, or activities, she tended to take a correspondingly relaxed position in an attempt to balance my firmness. With each indication of permissiveness on her part, I tended to tighten the reins to compensate. Inch by inch, we became polarized. The same thing happened in most decisions, until we found less and less common ground.

During our work in family therapy, a very astute

counselor picked up on our frequent use of the word *battle*. Indeed, the most stormy period of Portia's adolescent years seemed like a pitched battle. The territory shifted and the foes rotated according to the issue in dispute. The damage could have been caused only by a series of battles over territory, identity, authority, power, and the obvious lack of intimacy. Our therapist asked us to think about which issues were important to each of us and which battles we were willing to lose. I think for the first time I was willing to face the fact that I did not like the image itself. The therapist wisely pressed the issue and demanded that we use the image we ourselves had suggested. We followed his lead reluctantly and sorted out the issues most important to each of us, reached some compromises, and set out on the road to change in methodology — and imagery.

What may have been more important was the distaste we discovered we all had for the battle image itself. None of us felt comfortable with battles, with winning or losing. Yet, we knew some issues were so important to each of us that we would fight for them if we knew no other way. However, we discovered strength in our convictions and the possibilities of expressing them and upholding them through alternative methods. My wife and I began to see that we shared not only a sense of what was important but also some methods by which acceptable order could be maintained.

Parental leadership must always be authoritative and occasionally authoritarian. Effective and successful families are not democracies. Age, experience, and responsibility carry with them the necessity for order, order that is established and maintained for the well-being of the entire family and society at large. Even children, however, recognize when that order is vaguely defined and conflicted by parental disagreement. Our family's task in this restructuring was neither more nor less than two parents discovering which policies were nonnegotiable and how far we would go to maintain those policies. For example, we determined that we would not make an issue of clothing or grades. But we agreed that it was important for the girls to observe curfews and to be honest with us about where they were going and with whom. When that became clear for everyone, and the children recognized the security which derived from that kind of order, they accepted those policies with a sense of relief and eventual gratitude. The four of us then seemed free to allow nearly every other issue to be decided with flexibility and without anyone pushing to win or to defeat someone else. In that process the image of the battle simply faded unnoticed into the background. And the storms began to recede, or at least lessened in intensity.

Don't Take It Personally — Even If It Seems To Be Personal!

Rabbi Edwin H. Friedman, therapist and author of *Generation to Generation* (New York: Guilford Press, 1985), describes what he calls a "non-anxious presence" in leaders. What a far cry from storms and battles! A non-anxious presence does not retreat into silence or busyness or another room for the purpose of abdicating responsibility. A non-anxious presence is able to be wrong, to be imperfect, or simply to allow another person to take risks, make decisions, or fail.

I recall struggling not to take the choices, decisions, or even criticisms of my children personally, even when I knew they were directed more against me than toward their own good. Early in their childhood when their mother or I disciplined them or refused some wish, they responded with, "I hate you!" We were able then to answer quietly, "I know you do right now. I hope you won't hate me all the time." Or occasionally we would say, "Sometimes I don't like you very much either, but most of the time I like you a lot!"

I am still learning that my daughters choose an opinion, a direction, or a pathway different from what I would choose for them simply because they must exert their own individuality. Frequently I know what they are doing and must push back the hurt or disappointment with the knowledge that if they are to become mature, interdependent, and responsible adults, they must differentiate themselves. I have also watched as they have moved back toward much of what I hold to be important, not for my sake but because they have chosen what seems good to them.

I am still discovering that the storms which adolescents create are terribly threatening to them as well as to their parents, and that the rainbows are most beautiful and welcome in their aftermath.

CHAPTER IV

Time Is on Your Side

A PRAYER in the baby dedication ceremony used in the church I serve says, in part,

> We acknowledge them [the children]
> to be ours to guide,
> but not to own.

That early acknowledgment provides a perspective on the time span of primary parenting. After all, parents are required by necessity to provide care, protection, and oversight for their children during one-third or less of both their lives and their children's lives.

Some parents will laugh at such a suggestion. One or two generations back, says the wit, parents dreaded to see their youngsters leave home; now parents fear their youngsters will never leave home! Obviously, many children do stay home longer or move back home after college or in the middle of job changes or after their marriages have failed. For the most part, however, our children leave home between eighteen and twenty-two years of age and assume adult responsibilities. Parents then face more than one-third of their lives with lessened responsibilities for their children — indeed, in many cases with few responsibilities or none at all; they are free to enjoy their children, offer them encouragement and emotional support, and provide occasional assistance. During this period, the levels of responsibilities are determined more by parents than by their adult sons and daughters.

When parents recognize the time span of primary parenting responsibility, they gain perspective on the pressures of the more difficult periods of their children's growing-up process. Awareness of the limits that time places upon us works two ways. The relentlessness of clock and calendar suggests that no matter how difficult the period, it is not likely to last forever; and no matter how rewarding, fulfilling, and pleasurable the period, neither is it likely to last forever. I have taped to my office desk an age-yellowed card on which is written an ageless quip: "THIS TOO SHALL PASS!" That card reminds me not to take too seriously the times when life seems very bad or to allow to be too exhilarating those times when life seems absolutely wonderful. Most of us need help to maintain some balance of emotion and attitude.

The people in the Middle Ages of the Western world believed strongly in what was called the "wheel of fortune." The calendar never stopped, nor could any human being avoid the influences and the inevitability of both time and fortune. Everyone was thought to be tied, as it were, to that ceaselessly turning wheel. It might take one to the top, but sooner or later it would also carry the arrogant or even happy person to the bottom — and vice versa. Modern people know that life hardly takes such even and symmetrical turns, but the image serves to remind us that what goes around indeed seems to come around.

However we understand and measure the movement of time — in hours, years, or decades — both parents and children live and move under its restraints and compulsions. Think of all the references we make to time as our children are growing up. "Just a minute." "We're almost there." "Time for bed!" (which is often met with, "Why can't I stay up until this is over?") "You can't do that (or have that) until you're twelve (or sixteen or eighteen or twenty-one)." Surely it is a generalization, but parents seem always to be pleading with their small children to be patient; adolescents, in their own often bizarre ways, seem always to be begging their parents to be patient. In the parenting years, however, time really is on the side of everyone involved. That process of growing up requires time, and perhaps more patience than wisdom.

The Joys of One Time; The Stress of Another

My children grew up too fast. No, I don't think I rushed them intentionally, nor do I blame completely society's

79

pressuring them to hurry along. Some elements from both influenced the process. Parents tend unwittingly to expect their children to act like adults even before they become teenagers, be responsible, speak and think a decade ahead of their education and experience, manage money, and make all decisions with wisdom beyond their years. Such expectations are seldom out of line with our love and our dreams for them. My children grew up too fast because that is what children of our time do, perhaps what all children have always done. When we enjoy them, when they give us such pleasure, when each day brings surprises, fun, laughter, exploration, and warmth, we feel sad when our children begin to move away from us and start to create their own worlds.

"Do you remember the time we . . . ?" How those recollections multiply when we look through photograph albums and review reels and tapes of our children growing up! I recall a wedding rehearsal dinner at which the two sets of parents reviewed the couple's growing-up years. They used two slide projectors and screens, and in a brief but well-arranged chronology, they showed simultaneously pictures of the bride's and the groom's odysseys, beginning with the preschool years, moving on to the early/middle/older childhood events, showing highlights of the teen years, and finishing with their courtship period. Time moved very quickly in the review, and most of us commented that children seem to grow up too fast — both on projector screens and in real life.

Obviously, the further we are separated in time

from our children's early years, the more we tend to idealize the process and our attitudes. We push into the background the high fevers, the cuts and bruises, the tears over arithmetic problems and science projects, the teacher we had trouble with, the grief over a best friend who moved away. We forget the sleepless nights we spent caring for a sick child, and the vows we made never to permit another sleep-over or pajama party. We no longer remember the arguments about clothing or cleaning up messes or eating everything on the plate or who broke the vase.

Children are a great deal of work. Parenting requires a great deal of energy, money, and, of course, time! The early years of parenting furnish us with all sorts of fears about our children's health, education, and safety. Each step beyond the range of parental control raises concerns about the influence of others, from the neighborhood children to the adults in whose care the children are placed. The intellectual and emotional resources required in parenting test every adult, especially those in two-career families. Nevertheless, our children are so important to us and provide us with so much pleasure and pride that we tend to lose track of the steady tick of the clock and step of the calendar.

Then, all of a sudden, at some point we may or may not be able to identify, the clock stops; time appears to stand still. The child becomes a source of puzzlement at best and total disruption at worst. The costumes change. Dialogue and interchange become a series of diametric monologues and even harangues.

The emotional violins give way to discordant brass and throbbing percussion. Whatever orchestra we thought was our family seems more like the tuning process before the concert. The musical theater the parents designed so carefully and worked so hard to produce seems like a comedy of errors, or even a tragedy without resolution.

The impatient traveler who used to ask "Are we almost there?" now lashes out with the assertion that "I'll be glad when I'm sixteen (or eighteen or out of high school). I'm leaving and never coming back!" These threats that seem so harsh and final may make the parents feel panic-stricken — or prompt them to offer a caustic rejoinder to the effect that "You won't be any happier about that than I will!" When an eight- or nine-year-old threatens to run away and we offer to help him pack, solutions seem much simpler; when a six-teen-year-old issues the same threat, parents know he has the means to carry it out. The time to grow up and go away proves to be painful beyond imagination.

These are the years in which time seems like an endless issue. How late to stay out! How much time for homework! How much time with a boyfriend/girl-friend! How much time for a part-time job! How much time for sleep! How much time with the family! How much time to do some chores around the house! To the teenager, the clock seems like a prison guard.

Parents watch the clock as well. Who can sleep soundly until the car turns into the driveway? How does a parent remind the couple in the living room that the curfew has long since passed? How many times must a parent remind her that she is about to miss the school bus or be late for an appointment? How much nagging about practice time at the piano is counterproductive? A third wake-up call! A dreaded parent-teacher conference at three! Time is of the essence — the clock always moves, but the calendar seems to have stopped. It seems that parents of teenagers have to be stuck in this time struggle for several years! The hands of the clock go round and round, but all the days seem alike! A weary, frustrated, and melancholy mother commented rhetorically to her husband, "Will we ever be happy again?"

The most dramatic moment in suspended time that I remember in Portia's adolescent years came just at the turning point in our attempts at some specific conflict resolution. At that juncture none of us knew just what the future held for us. We had renegotiated the functioning process of our family system as best we could. We had each decided on which issues (called "battles") we were willing to lose, and on which issues we were unwilling to compromise. Inasmuch as everyone had "won" some points and "conceded" others, we determined that we could live together, work together, and strive for whatever progress we would discover that seemed possible in the process.

Clearly, whatever seam divided the fabric of childhood from that of adolescence had apparently become quite pronounced in appearance. To use another image, we had reached a part of our journey that had seemed suspended in time — although it was not! — because the terrain had become much more demanding. Close friends who knew of our pain, who had been through difficult times with their own teenagers, reminded us carefully and gently that time really was on our side. We respected them and could see that many of their sons and daughters had made their way through rough terrain of their own and had assumed admirably their roles as responsible, interdependent, and mature adults. Intellectually, we accepted our friends' encouragement; emotionally, we appreciated their concern. We had little idea and less optimism about what the future actually held for us, however, but we knew we had crossed the line between childhood and adulthood. Old ways of doing things were being traded for new ones, both for Portia and for Jessica.

The most poignant moment I remember occurred in our backyard. Portia and I were outdoors, sitting on the pile of firewood. Practically every conversation we had had for two years had been strained and defensive. We were trying to talk and to listen, but for several months our efforts had been careful and reserved. I felt a deep need to tell her something about my pain and my hope. I told her about the little girl I remembered, loved, and raised. I told her who I had thought that person was, and the joy she had given me. I told her in an image that was terribly powerful for me, and I can only imagine for her, the most painful thing I had ever said: I told her I thought that little girl had died!

After I said that, there was a long silence. I can do no more than speculate about Portia's feelings. I am sure she was stunned. I am equally sure she could not have known how deeply I had loved that little girl. For me it was like mourning; for her it must have been like reading her own obituary. After a while, I resumed my confession, even more agonizingly.

I tried to explain something of my grief, realizing all during the conversation/monologue that grief cannot be explained. I tried to communicate to her how I had come to think about the necessity of the death of certain aspects of the past, that I could willingly let go of those; but I related as best I could the awful pain I felt at having lost the child who had been so dear to me. I waited again for some response; none came. That moment was then sealed in my being. To this day we have not discussed it. But at that time, as we sat on the woodpile, we seemed to have been in a graveyard. But then, what response could she have made!

After several more minutes of silence, I told her I believed in resurrection, rebirth, new life. I did not know this new person now with me, and perhaps I never even knew the little girl either. Perhaps the person she was in my consciousness had never really existed, but I was hopeful of some resurrection of that person — surely not that identical person, but whoever she had become or was becoming — and I promised my best effort to lay aside expectations and let her show me who she was and would be. The very effort it took to say what I felt weighed heavily upon me. I was caught in a moment in which all time stood still, and I was sad and frightened. Still, my daughter made no response. What is a seventeen-year-old to say in the face of her own death? I have little doubt that her grief was nearly as deep as my own and her future as uncertain for her as my own was for me.

The moment overflowed with power — the power both of sadness and of hope. I tried to let her know that I accepted my share of responsibility for our suffering as a family and for her pain individually, about which I realized I knew very little. I tried to emphasize my commitment to her, to our family and our relationship, and to the effort required to rebuild what obviously had been badly damaged, to heal what was terribly broken. To this day I have no idea how she processed that confession and pledge from her father. Nevertheless, I believe that event in time-standing-still was a hingepin of my acceptance that, to paraphrase the Apostle, "old things had passed away; all things [must] become new."

In recent years I have often wondered if young people who are caught in time that seems to stand still feel forced to create such havoc in their homes that parents reach a point of being almost glad to see them go, willing to let them go. In some cases, dramatic efforts to reach adulthood are required if parents are to loosen their grip and teenagers are to take the risk of launching out into a difficult world. The turmoil of these sometimes painful years can provide the impetus, the energy, and the will to renegotiate relationships, adjust expectations, and even change radically the way entire families make decisions and manage conflict. Indeed, when the system fails, survival instincts cry out for a new system. If parents can see time as an ally, these painful seams between two periods in life, this rough terrain on a difficult journey, can offer new beginnings that may prove to be rewarding long-term.

A Time of Hope and Renegotiation

During our most conflicted time, my family had essentially two options. First, we could have chosen to patch up the broken system and maintain appearances until our daughters left for college. Such a choice would have meant that we would determine the minimal requirements for reaching some liberation for all of us. To continue the battle image, negotiating a "treaty" would allow everyone to win some and lose some so we could co-exist. But that option was simply unacceptable. To live for five more years on pins and needles, awaiting the next explosion or working our way through the minefields of dissatisfaction, would have taken its toll on four people who had always committed themselves to some levels of excellence.

The second option required a new way of life and a great deal of hard work. The four of us agreed to some new directions, although my wife and I would be called upon to change the most, to model the risk of being and doing on a higher and more cooperative level. For us, passivity would have created a burden worse than the conflicts we had recently experienced. All four of us knew at some level that if we were to maintain any acceptable semblance of "family," we could not stand still or pretend that our problems were temporary, the fault of children growing up.

I understood that I had contributed substantially to our corporate malfunction because I had chosen to be overly directive and too active in shaping our children's lives, controlling at a level they found oppressive. I knew my own approach to parenting had not worked for them. I further realized that the time had come for my wife and me to make some adjustments in our own relationship, based upon who each of us had been becoming rather than on who we were twenty-five years earlier when we had met and eventually married. I committed myself to change. I believe my wife made commitments similarly demanding of her.

That resurrection image became increasingly powerful. As sad as I felt, every day and most of every day, I knew myself to be theologically oriented. Hope was part of the fiber of my being. I reflected constantly upon such theological categories as repentance and forgiveness, redemption and salvation, providence and grace. I knew instinctively that death is a part of new life and that on some level something of my self had to die in order to be reborn, even as I had suggested to Portia. For a time, I must have felt something like Mary at the tomb of Jesus: she was so overwhelmed by grief and pain that she could not see light or hope, or even the one she thought she had lost. Yet, she was at the tomb. She was in a place where her risen Lord could find her. I was intensely conscious of such images.

Time seemed to have stood completely still for me, and yet, time really did seem to be on our side. I recall a breakthrough in which I realized that we had stopped talking about what was wrong among us, what was not working, and had begun to look to the future. That breakthrough involved the purchase of a car for Portia. It became a symbol of her impetus toward the future, in cooperation with her family.

She was seventeen, a senior in high school, active in the theater program. Her after-school rehearsals and part-time job impressed upon us the need for another car in the family. Almost as soon as we began to look seriously, we discussed a shared purchase arrangement. She would contribute some money; we would contribute the rest. As the arrangement developed, she paid $200 and agreed to provide her own gasoline. Her mother and I invested $1600. Almost immediately her world expanded and the level of trust between us improved. She saw my willingness to participate in meeting her need; in her eyes, that represented a major change in me. In the past I had expressed opposition to teenagers owning cars while they are in high school. My alteration of a previously firm stance indicated to her that there was a new direction both in the family and in her own life. Although the car we located had been driven more than 100,000 miles, it had been well cared for. Portia was as proud of it as if it had been a brand-new sports car. Both literally and symbolically, that car carried us toward the future; it became one of the means by which our family became unstuck. The clock and the calendar seemed to move again, albeit very slowly.

A second impetus toward the future was provided by helping Portia make her plans for college. Our family discussed her options and set out to visit a half-dozen colleges and universities. For families experiencing little or no conflict, such a process is normal and exciting within the boundaries of expectations that parents have for the development of their sons and daughters. This process may even represent a turning point for them, an essential set of rituals. For our family, however, the discussions about college were significant in a different way; they were as welcome as applause because they were discussions about something, anything, rather than arguments or silence. For us the visits to colleges represented a giant step forward because we were acting as though a future existed for Portia and for our family.

Life with any person caught in the throes of depression seems to stand still. Verbal expressions of the hopelessness and pointlessness of life overwhelm everything and everyone else. The language of sadness includes very little vocabulary about the future. That is why the preparations for college — touring campuses, poring over catalogues, and writing application essays — were for us as exciting as a trip to Disneyland.

During this period of emerging hopefulness, one more particular and spontaneous statement occurred, another special moment frozen in time. I remember the highway, the place on that highway, the time of day. In some sense, it now seems like the first ray of sunshine I had seen in many months. We had visited our second campus in as many days and planned to tour a third the next day. As we drove back to our accommodations for the evening, I told Portia that I regretted so much what had happened to us during the past couple of years, and that choosing colleges and being accepted in a college of her choice could have been so much easier had we all done things differently. She responded calmly but quickly, "I can't do anything about the past, and I've made up my mind not to let the past control me. I can only go on from where I am."

I heard her words as a kind of admonition to me, but more than that, I heard her say for the first time in a long time that there really would be a tomorrow for her. As it turns out, she spoke prophetically, because the next four years seemed to pick up steam and flew by at an accelerated pace. Time was again moving in its appointed rhythm!

Families in the midst of transition, especially when that transition involves an adolescent, may feel stuck for a long time. They may feel like every day is the same. Whatever is "out there" for others is impossible for them. Nevertheless, the way out is nearly always through. If a family patiently and doggedly remains in some sort of therapy and works hard at changing attitudes and unsatisfactory patterns of relating to one another, a turning point will one day surprise them. It may come in a conversation, in some kind of planning, in some significant resolution or change. But it will nearly always come as the family or one member of the family turns decisively to the future.

One aspect of change, healing, and hope is assessment. What is wrong? What doesn't work? What damage has been done? How do we divide up the causes and responsibilities? A good counselor can help a family explore those issues. In the process, however, some new directions must emerge. And they will. Adults would like to believe the change that occurs can be attributed to the natural growing-up process of the adolescent and his or her increasing responsibility. I am no longer convinced that we as adults can leave it at that. Yes, to grow up is to change, but simply trading faddish clothes for more adult garments is not enough. Replacing posters of rock singers with framed poetry and nature scenes falls short. Hostility in youth-to-adult relationships may give way to courtesy and accommodation without moving toward real maturity. It's not enough for the adolescents to change; the parents must change too. During this period of turmoil we as adults simply cannot lay all the family tensions at the feet of adolescents; nor should we assume that when they "grow up," everything will be well again.

Somewhere along the way I realized not only that I had to change with the rest of my family, but also that I really wanted to do things differently. Two factors pulled me in that direction and actually provided some impetus in the process.

The first of these influences, strangely enough, was exhaustion, weariness, my own depression. As Portia began to make plans, to move ahead, I found myself without energy. Worry, guilt, regret, and my professional work weighed heavily upon my shoulders. Ironically, my drivenness had always kept my mind and body in such high gear that I had had little time for self-examination. My confidence allowed for very little in the way of second-guessing or assessment. Only when I withered in the heat of a fire I could no longer control would I stop and allow the clock and calendar to run at their own appointed pace. I felt like an accident victim in a body cast: all I could do was lie in traction and think. Again, what seemed all bad had a positive side. Because I had less to say, others in the family were more able to speak. Because I had less energy to do things for everyone else, others in the family were able to make decisions and do things their own way. Time that seemed to stand still for me had begun to move forward for the rest of my family. Hence, the second influence.

Just as I had more or less carried the other family members along in my own designs for many years, they began to carry me along. For a significant period of time, our family was reconstituted into four people, each doing his or her own thing. We related (although uncomfortably) and discussed what we had to deal with, but generally we went our own ways. I found myself responding more than initiating, helping more than directing. Part of that method of functioning was intentional; I had said repeatedly that I needed to back off because of my absence of energy and because I felt terribly guilty for the sadness that existed in my family. What seemed like a backing off in a negative environment proved to be a healthy allowance of space that gave us the room we needed to reconstruct our relationships.

Portia's depression and hospitalization, Jessica's sense of guilt because she had spotted the difficulty before her parents and had served as the "keeper of the secret," parents without a workable plan — all had served to undermine what my wife and I had imagined to be a perfect family. When time seemed to stand still for us all, and especially for me, I was able to allow the others to move toward some future and pull me along with them. I suspect I was the last of the four of us to rediscover genuine optimism.

Time has indeed proven to be an ally, but I have concluded that simply waiting for children to grow up solves very few problems. Had we as a family, and I as a parent, refused to change our own ways of thinking, feeling, acting, and relating, we would probably have grown a few years older without the kind of rebirth we experienced. Families who choose to adjust their methods of functioning only enough to get through a crisis or to get their children grown and out on their own may simply be covering up a smoldering fire that will flare up again under other critical circumstances. My family chose the difficult road of change, reconstruction, renegotiation, and yes . . . resurrection!

I am told that the dual Chinese characters for the word *crisis* mean "danger" and "opportunity," respectively. When time seems to stand still for families in trouble, it may make them feel endangered, imperiled — but that suspension of time may be a gift, an opportunity for them to reassess their relationship. At the very least it is a suggestion that the family or some part of the life of the family is not working for everyone. Such tensions and the suspension of time may be a warning and a call to transformation. We could easily have accepted Portia's physical problems as the total cause of her distress and our family's difficulties. We did not discover those problems, however, until we had determined that there were some more basic flaws in our family system. Time, which proved very much on our side, eventually suggested to us that the severity of our difficulties had been exacerbated by a situation that we had no hand in creating; however, we could not ignore at some level our responsibility as a family and as individuals within that family. Most of all, I could not control the clock and calendar if I was sincere about renegotiating a new way of being family.

We chose the hard work of restructuring, reconstructing, and renegotiating something different because we knew we had reached a point of imminent chaos, had developed the behavior and attitudes of destructiveness. And, true to the clock and calendar, the task continues. I am increasingly aware that no battle (there's that metaphor again!) stays won. When I or other family members face stress common to relationships, the old patterns reassert themselves and prove tempting. After all, the human organism maintains its gravitational pull toward behavior it knows best!

I must catch myself now and again when I slip into patterns of controlling, directing, and shaping, and setting goals for others. I must stop myself and listen to what our daughters say and be sure I have heard them before I offer an opinion or serve up a directive. I must choose carefully those issues and areas in which I need to be authoritative without being authoritarian.

Time continues to move forward, and just as surely as time was on our side in the midst of our family's struggles, so time can be on our side in the future — providing we choose to continue the process of moving away from mediocrity and toward some sort of excellence in our relationships.

CHAPTER V

Parents Need Help

Significant Others and Community

I RECALL that as the day of Portia's birth drew near, I sensed an increasing emotional investment being made by our extended family, our closest friends, and especially by the members of the church I served as minister. One exchange now seems like a summary of what was happening in the process. After a church meeting one evening, a member who was also a social friend waited until everyone else had gone. She was the only daughter of a widow in the church, unmarried and devoted to her elderly mother. The two of them had taken their young minister under their wings and provided encouragement and support for my wife and me. Usually she was full of teasing and fun, but on this night she was serious.

"I want to offer you something," she said, "but I don't want you to feel obligated to take it."

I nodded a response and waited.

97

"It's my baby bed. I have it in the car, and you're welcome to take it and look it over. But I won't be offended if you decide you don't need it."

I said I would really like to look at it and that I was sure I would be honored to have it. She went around to the car, unlocked the trunk, and there it was, unassembled — a little more than fifty years old, the hardware a bit rusted and the paint in poor condition. I thought to myself, "How could I possibly get this bed in usable condition for our baby?" Still, I removed the bed from the car, telling her how much I appreciated her offer. I promised to take it into the house and assemble it, and then let her know what my wife and I thought about it.

As I walked from the parking lot to the parsonage, I figured I had a problem. I knew the bed would need a new paint job and some new hardware, and I had neither the time nor the inclination for such a job. Yet, I knew what this bed symbolized, and I wanted that connectedness with the church, our friends, and the past. I decided to see what it would take to restore it. I immediately called a woodworker/friend over to see it, explaining my delicate situation. He took out his pocketknife and scraped a little of the paint off the wood, then a little more paint, then a little more.

"Curly maple!" he said. "A clear finish would really set it off. You get the paint off and sand it down, and I'll put the finish on for you."

The next day I called our benefactor and told her that my wife and I would like to keep the bed and that we wanted to refinish it. She was delighted and I was overwhelmed! In the end I invested more than a hundred hours of work in that bed. But as I worked on it, I thought more about what it meant. As I have thought back on this incident, I have become increasingly aware of how that piece of furniture would become a symbol of both continuity and community.

That fifty-year-old bed would be a symbolic tie between two families related by faith in God and by friendship. That bed would suggest my family's place in the context of the church community. That bed would cradle not one daughter, but two. And if either or both of them have children, it will probably be used again and again. That bed is one of many symbols of continuity and community with which my nuclear family is still connected.

We are hardly alone in such connectedness. Every family has some piece of furniture, some artifact, some keepsake, some story that serves as a reminder of both continuity and community. New parents may feel like the only couple ever to have undertaken the tasks and experienced the joys of parenting, but connections like that bed bring into focus a much larger picture.

New parents may not develop a comparatively full understanding and appreciation of such relationships for a long time; they will unfold, however. The process of refinishing that bed opened the door of understanding for me just a crack. The next level of understanding came the morning of the birth of that first child. I had been awake all night; my wife had been undergoing intense labor throughout the wee hours of that morning. When the baby finally arrived and I held her for the first time, the weariness, anxiety, and emotion of the moment flashed before me the realization that this new person presented a responsibility that my wife and I might not be capable of assuming alone. My prayer, "God, I want to be a good parent," was a confession of both desire and need. I left the hospital and drove the ten miles to our home as first light broke. "We're going to need a lot of help," I thought. I had no idea how right I was! Yet that help had already begun to appear; the baby bed was a reminder that we were not alone in our task.

Our children were born into a world vastly different from the world I had known as a child. Their children will experience a world still more different. Each generation argues about the stresses upon both parents and children. Who has it more difficult may be less important than whether or not each generation is able to adapt to those stresses and needs. The supreme gift, however, will be the ability of each new generation to recognize those human needs and resources that never change. Among those resources are significant others and "community."

By now most of us are weary of discussions about the shift from agrarian to urban/suburban living, the effects of a transient society in separating us from our families of origin, and the power of air conditioning and television to keep our doors and attention closed to our immediate neighbors. We are just now beginning to face the further isolating factor of the tools and toys of the electronic world: computers, video games, telephone answering machines, and fax machines. "Others" tend increasingly to be voices, images, and print; "community" tends to mean very loosely connected acquaintances.

Contemporary parents are indeed aware of the need of their families for a network of involved, caring, helpful relatives and friends. Yet, as the demands of parenting have increased, resources seem to have diminished. The over-fifty group tell the younger parents those stories about farming communities, small and close-knit neighborhoods (where the houses were smaller and closer together, the windows and doors were open, and the kids were in and out of everybody's house!), churches and schools that were the centers of social life, and extended families whose members lived within walking distance of one another. Perhaps all that is overstated, but not by much.

I still recall with a smile an incident that occurred in one of the two neighborhoods I remember from my childhood. On a summer day I walked with a couple of playmates down an alley between the backyards of our neighbors' houses. The three of us were talking loudly, laughing and joking. I must have used a four-letter word! One of the neighbor ladies, working in her backyard, opened her gate, stepped into the alley, grabbed my arm, stared into my eyes, and said, "Wayne Price, if I ever hear you talk like that again, I'll spank you on the spot and take you home and your mother will spank you again!" She would have, and my mother would have too! There were parents and relatives and neighbors and teachers and fellow church members and storekeepers and service providers who believed raising children should be a cooperative venture. I believe I was and am better for that system. And that is the system which is now little more than a memory.

Those days are gone, and for better or worse, they are not likely to return. However, it is less important to lament the passing of old methodologies and more important to search for new significant persons and community. Each set of parents and each single parent faces the issue of the human resources network necessary to help our children on the road to maturity, responsibility, and interdependency.

What Kind of Community?

"Community" of the sort that is capable of and willing to participate in the task of nurturing and guiding children must be more than a neighborhood. Simply because people live in houses and apartments a few feet apart doesn't mean any bonding has occurred. The news media report almost daily some case of violence — abuse and even murder — in neighborhoods where the residents hardly know one another. "He seemed like a nice man." "They were pleasant, but they hardly spoke to anyone." "Everybody in the neighborhood works, so there isn't much time to socialize." On and on go the comments suggesting that people live close to one another, and yet far away.

The problem children encounter in their need for direction, affirmation, and companionship is not so much that they are misdirected as that they are left to their own devices. "Latch-key children," children raised on television and video games, children without an available extended family — these situations open doors to all sorts of deficiencies in the growing-up years. Perhaps the greatest deficiency is that children must become their own parents. Such need not be the case if a family works continually at creating and renewing community as an alternative to simply living in a neighborhood.

Community literally means "at one with." This is far more than "neighborhood," a place where a number of families live in proximity to one another. Community involves people in interaction, in some level of shared responsibility, in an extended time frame. The day a family moves into their house, they become a part of the neighborhood; becoming part of a community always requires investment of time and other resources.

Parents who are separated from their own families of origin, extended families, and circles of lifelong friends face difficult choices. They can either attempt to be a self-sufficient community for their children and travel frequently to the communities they left behind, or they can find or create new communities. Fortunately, children have a way of forcing parents to create and expand their circles of friends. As they do so, they introduce their parents to potential members of such a created network of surrogate families.

How many of us remember when our children got to the point at which they resented those long drives to the grandparents' homes at Christmastime! They wanted to stay in their own homes, visit with their own friends, observe their own emerging traditions. How many of us count among our friends the families to which our children introduced us! We have all met fascinating adults through the playmates of our youngsters, and in some cases we will maintain those friendships even after our children grow up and leave home. Our children really do influence the makeup of our community network.

Whatever the source of our communities — church, school, neighborhoods, social groups — children teach us how much work is involved and how essential such communities are to our own families. The same kind of bonding that occurs in nuclear families is required in the creation and development of every other kind of social unit. Time and energy are always primary building blocks. Openness and listening, decision making, occasional conflict management, flexibility, celebration, and affirmation all require both primary attention and some premium energy. And the children are involved in both the need and the network.

As I reflect upon the experience of my family in the process of developing surrogate family and community, the high points have to do with our children. I recall many requests from each of them to invite the family of one of their friends to have dinner with us. They requested year by year that we entertain various schoolteachers. Nearly every weekend one of them wanted us to visit or host some family with whom we were connected. Perhaps the outstanding image of these visits is Jessica standing at the door, as guests were preparing to leave our home or we were preparing to leave someone else's home, crying bitterly because she did not want to conclude the visit.

Developing a network of families into our own smaller community was absolutely necessary for us. My position as minister of a church offered immediately the possibility for close relationships, but it also heightened the necessity for them. Because my responsibilities on Sundays and holidays required that I not leave town, we were seldom able to spend Christmas, Easter, Thanksgiving, or other national holidays with our extended families. In a very real sense, the church became our primary extended family: surrogate grandparents and aunts, uncles, and cousins were always available to us through the church. Natural grandparents and aunts, uncles, and cousins had to be visited as we could make arrangements around official duties.

Many families experience similar predicaments because of the distance between themselves and relatives. They may lament their dilemma; they may also see it as an opportunity to expand their network of relationships, thus enriching their lives and providing additional resources for their children. My family has been admitted into the inner circles of many families at some of their most intimate celebrations. We have shared holiday dinners, anniversaries, traditions, and rituals with many families; these have widened our own perspective and continue to enrich our lives.

Nevertheless, for all my awareness of the need for these friends and the richness they have brought to my own family, one reservation on my part limited what community could have done better for our children. My own self-reliance and defective capacity for trust established some unnecessary boundaries for our children. In those long growing-up years, my wife and I together were away from our girls overnight no more than two or three times. In all those years we employed babysitters very rarely and generally out of necessity rather than for our own pleasure and recreation.

As the "shaper" of our children's lives, I assumed that no one could care for our children as well as my wife and I could. We took them with us many times when they would have enjoyed staying home. We planned no time away and alone for our own rest, pleasure, recreation, and renewal. I was determined to be a good (perfect) parent, which meant being present and attentive. In retrospect, through that wonderful vision called hindsight, I realize how much others could have contributed to our children in our absence, and how we could have sent them the positive message that our relationship with one another was just as important as our relationship with them. Even more important may have been the lessons they could have learned about their own self-reliance as well as about a broader circle of trust.

I now wonder how serious I really was about how much we as parents needed a real and interdependent community. I suspect that I wanted a convenient community, but with unevenly shared responsibilities. Like all methodologies, however, mine was called into question when it no longer worked well for our family. The time came when we were literally compelled to look to others for more intensive support and deeper wisdom than we could find within ourselves.

When Crisis Deepens Connectedness

Just as the adolescent years challenged many other presuppositions and methods of parenting, so those critical years expanded my presuppositions about community. In fact, while I continue to assess my attitudes during those years when our children were small, I suspect my sense of surrogate family had more to do with neighborhood than with community. I enjoyed social and casual friendships but believed I needed little help with the more intense responsibilities connected with parenting. I believed that I knew better than anyone else what our children needed, and by implication that I was more capable than anyone else of providing for those needs.

The time came, however, when what I thought I knew and what I had been doing no longer worked. Those years of our children's adolescence seem now like a homemade boat that starts to list in a less-than-gale-

107

force wind. Our family's crises have not been nearly as severe as the difficulties faced by many other families during the critical teen years of their children. Yet, when parents believe that they're doing everything exactly right, a storm of moderate proportions causes them to feel like they're being blown off the edge of the world.

Fortunately, we had not done everything wrong. Our family had in place a network of many caring and competent friends. If I had not trusted them as deeply in the past as I might have, I realized I needed them in crisis. The first person to whom I turned when Portia's depression became frightening was a seminary peer who directed a mental health center in our area. I will say much more about his contributions to our progress in the next chapter. Suffice it to say here that he was my professional colleague and casual friend; he became an essential figure in whose hands our family placed our present and our future. He guided us carefully and sensitively through many months of stabilizing, learning, changing, and growing. He did so both as a professional and as a friend, but I believe primarily as a friend.

At this point I need to say something about vulnerability as a doorway to self-awareness and progress in family relationships. Perhaps the poorest parents in the world are the ones who think they know everything about parenting, the ones who are certain that nothing will go wrong in their particular family system. Perhaps the best parents in the world are those who recognize the precariousness of human existence and the unpredictability of children when they are growing up — or grown — and who themselves are willing to grow and learn along with their children.

Sailors learn their best lessons in storms, almost nothing in a gentle, consistent breeze. Crises, threats to our security, challenges to our presuppositions, the failures of systems we believed were nearly perfect — all tend to soften our rigidity and render us incredibly teachable. And vulnerability heightens our appreciation of the other hands on deck. All of a sudden they are more than weekend acquaintances, next-door neighbors; they are part of our very survival system.

The most difficult thing I ever had to do was to admit Portia to a hospital, a ward with locks on the doors. I remember sitting in the admitting office, tears streaming down my face, struggling to answer the clerk's questions. The information the clerk was after seemed so mundane in the face of my internal questions. Would Portia attempt suicide? How severely depressed was she? What was the cause — and what had I contributed to it? Would she recover? I cried the entire half-hour drive home. I cried at some point every day for weeks. And in my vulnerability, I learned some things about community, about a network of caring friends. I learned a great deal about myself. Most of all, in my vulnerability I was gradually able to change directions.

My primary support system was "my group." Five years earlier, another friend and I had helped to form a seven-man "support group" that had met for an hour and a half each and every week. How prophetic the

rationale for the group turned out to be! At the formative meeting I told the other men, "Life is great for me
right now, but I know that won't always be the case.
When the bottom falls out for me, I want to have some
caring friends around me." The others echoed my sen-
timents. We made a verbal contract on the particulars:
weekly meetings, commitment to faithful attendance,
no facilitator, open agenda, support rather than analysis.
All seven of us were professionals who worked in some
area of human services.

Week by week through the long autumn of my
family's intense struggle, I met with my friends. I felt
safe, encouraged, and supported by each of them personally and by the group as a unit. They offered little
advice and a great deal of compassion. More importantly, they saw to it that we dealt with other issues
besides my own. The weeks turned into months, and
progress in my family seemed most often slow and
sometimes nonexistent. True, some changes did occur.
Following thirty days in the hospital, Portia returned
home and went back to school. But all of us in the
family walked on eggs, not sure of ourselves or the
future.

In the course of my own long struggle to cope,
understand, and change, another member of the group
was diagnosed with cancer and would live only six more
months. The intensity of our meetings, first because of
the level of my needs and then because of his illness,
were such that the group grew in importance for all of
us. My friend's struggle with cancer helped to put the

crisis of my own family into perspective, yet my ongoing struggles were always dealt with as thoroughly as his needs. My group became community to me in the purest sense.

Another part of my network during the period of my most intense pain proved the most serendipitous — my colleagues on the church staff and a few close friends among the laity became my ministers. I had been their pastor, their leader, the one who tried to give to them. In my need, the roles were reversed. The day after Portia was admitted to the hospital, I met with the church staff. I explained to them in detail what was happening and told them I could make no promises about the quality of leadership I would be able to provide. I asked them to protect my confidence inasmuch as I chose for the time being not to tell the entire church anything about what was happening.

I told them openly that I was very embarrassed that the excellent parent I had believed I was no longer seemed so excellent. (That embarrassment was the primary reason for not relating my family's difficulty to the entire church.) Neither did I want to call widespread attention to our daughter at that point. I wanted the professionals to be able to do their work without attention from anyone except those Portia chose to summon.

For several weeks I went about my work rather mechanically, seeing only people I needed to see, working often behind the closed doors of my study, and having my staff take care of a number of things. They did a great deal of my administrative work for me and covered the necessary details when I was out of the office. I was sad, numb, depressed, and not very optimistic about life itself. Most of all, I was afraid for Portia.

I also confided in a rather significant group of church friends and leaders. Almost daily one or more of them telephoned, stopped by my study, invited me to lunch, wrote notes of encouragement, and offered help. Several with whom Portia chose to communicate provided her with academic tutoring, flowers, notes, and messages. Support was competent, constant, and most of all compassionate.

Again, during those weeks of uncertainty, the encouragement and help I received from my colleagues and friends in the church proved invaluable. More than that, a broadening and deepening of real community occurred without my being aware of it. My vulnerability allowed others to care for me in the short term and help me with necessary changes in my style of parenting and relating to others over the longer term.

As I was discovering a deeper level of community for myself, one couple emerged as particularly helpful to Portia. They recognized her need for adult companionship outside her own family circle and stepped in to fill that need. They had been close friends for several years; they were a part of the family support system. But they also knew Portia needed some help, and they responded. They invited her to their home, offered academic tutoring, and maintained steady contact. We were delighted that she chose to accept their specific offers.

My wife and I expressed very directly our appreciation for their involvement in her life, and we realized immediately that in responding to Portia they were also helping to care for us. What I had believed we as parents were completely capable of doing for our children proved an impossible dream; I was developing an increasing awareness of the importance of others in the lives of our children, of the importance of their participation not only in birthday celebrations and dinner parties but also in the major crises of our children's lives. I was beginning to realize that I could not be everything to them; in fact, by attempting to be everything, I had become a major part of their problem. I had to learn to trust others and accept my own limitations. It was a hard lesson, one gracefully offered by our friends.

As Portia began to rediscover a sense of her future and develop renewed hope, my wife and I began to recognize that Jessica also needed her own adult friend. From the beginnings of our upheaval, we had realized something of the silent burden she had borne — aware, earlier than we had been, of both the nature and the intensity of our family's dysfunction. She could not have verbalized much of it, and she chose to be the keeper of the secret that everything was not all right. She continues to bear some of the burden of those difficult times, but she does so exceedingly well.

My wife and I talked with Jessica and asked her if she felt she needed an adult friend. She agreed that she would like someone to be with, talk to, claim as her own outside our family — and she was quick to name the person. I met with the woman; she is a middle-aged parent of grown children, a grandparent, a woman of deep faith and gentle disposition, a fine listener. When I explained our need, she did just what I knew she would: she acknowledged that I was asking a great deal because she would take the arrangement seriously if she decided she could commit herself to it. A week later she called to say she would like to take Jessica under her wing.

That relationship has grown steadily. The two of them shop, go out for lunch, or sit in her home and talk. Neither of them tells my wife or me what they talk about, but we are always aware of the positive attitude these times seem to engender in Jessica. I suspect the two of them will remain good friends for the rest of their lives, no matter where Jessica lives after college.

My wife and I have watched as both girls have interacted on deeper levels with several other adult friends — teachers, church staff members, Sunday School leaders. In some respects that interaction is part of the normal process of their becoming adults themselves; they have always had adult friends, and it is natural for them to rely increasingly upon such people as they mature. After all, most children deepen their friendships outside the home as they grow older; and as their lives become more complicated, they depend upon those adult friends for help of many sorts. Nevertheless, I am convinced that I had to turn our daughters loose so that they could reach out more widely and more deeply. They are doing so, and I feel that the yoke of responsibility is lighter for me because others are sharing it with us.

The Most Difficult Lesson; The Greatest Gift

I had always seen myself as a helping person, but one who seldom needed major help. Almost without being aware of it, I had wanted our children to be independent, analytical in their thinking, and willing to challenge the norm and move in their own directions. Yet, my approach to parenting by its very nature hindered any such direction. Because I tended to help too much, to be too directive as a parent, the girls lived with a confusing message: on the one hand, be independent and think for yourselves, and on the other hand, Dad will tell you what to do and how to do it!

The struggles that Portia accepted voluntarily — to challenge the system, move in her own direction, seek her own levels — were unwitting judgments on her father's inconsistent methodology and vision, since those struggles contributed in part to her depression. Friends and other helping persons who offered assistance not as casual acquaintances but as vital and essential members of our community enabled me to begin the difficult process of change. I began to feel myself letting go of some responsibility, relaxing my excessively controlling hold on the girls; I began to learn how to be more responsive, less directive.

Early on, I did much of my backing off with a mixture of emotions — great sadness, fear for Portia's well-being, anger, guilt about all that I had done poorly or incorrectly. The healing power of deep friendships enabled me increasingly to relax and enjoy the process and occasionally to see the humor in it. Early on, my friends offered compassion and support for my shaken life: they listened, shared time and table, helped as they could. As time passed, they were able to help me interpret what was happening, how I was seeing things differently, how life might develop down some distant tomorrow.

One of the girls' adult friends said to me one evening, "You wanted her to be her own person. It looks to me like that's just what she's trying to be." I answered defensively, "But I didn't expect it to be this traumatic." Much, much later, I was able to to see that I had made it difficult by holding on too tightly. Our friends had made it easier by holding all of us more gently.

CHAPTER VI

Time Out

Where To Go for Help

THE normal struggles for families with adolescent children can be stressful and unsettling at the very least. When parents face a crisis in the growing-up process of their children, shock and sometimes panic take over. Your sixteen-year-old is being held at the police station! A friend brings your teenager home because she's gotten sick from drinking too much! The hospital telephones to say your son is all right, but that he has been in an accident! You wait through the long night and into the morning hours for your youngster to return home, only to realize she has run away!

No matter how well we believe we function as parents, the chances are overwhelming that we will face both the normal stresses and one or more major crises during our children's adolescence. Some of these difficulties will threaten the lives of the young people we love so much; other conflicts and tensions will signal the presence of problems we either knew nothing about or chose to ignore; every threat to our calm and orderly family routine seems to call into account our stewardship as parents.

We may choose to deny deeper issues by giving our attention and energy to solving the problem at hand. A lecture about drinking and a week without the car! Some weeping and hand-wringing! Threats and recriminations! If, however, we are able to control knee-jerk reactions, we may be able to ask ourselves if there is a message behind the event. Is the real problem the improper behavior, or is something wrong on a much deeper level? If we read them properly, such dramatic actions can tell us that something is not right; the actions even contain hints about what that "something" might be. At the very least, we can see that what seemed to have worked just a couple of years earlier no longer works. That normal and rewarding period of childhood seems to have become little more than a memory. Extreme kinds of behavior — substance abuse, sexual promiscuity, a series of major traffic violations, poor academic performance, bizarre dress — may be the youngster's way of screaming to the parents that something in his or her life is missing or has gone terribly wrong.

In our frustration and anger as parents, we may increase the level of advice-giving, nagging, and lecturing. We may choose to tighten the reins of control we seem to be losing. We may shout our own threats and ultimatums. And we will probably be greeted by further withdrawal, more extreme behavior, and defiance. Each time the parents increase the pressure and the teenager intensifies the reaction, the family becomes more severely polarized. Fortunately, many more effective options are available to us.

Where To Turn in a Family Storm

When our children are having problems, the first resource is the family itself — provided the family has the courage to look inside itself at both the factors that contribute to those problems and the strengths necessary for improvement and change. My own regret as a parent is not so much what I did poorly as that I waited far too long to look inside myself. For as long as two years, a variety of hints, tips, and signals went right past me before I began to realize that what my wife and I had been doing as parents no longer met our family's needs. As often seems the case with adolescents, the "acting out," the distress signals, become increasingly dramatic and strident until somebody is willing to admit that something is not right. It was not until Portia's distress signals — unacceptable behavior, depression, and hints of suicide — reached the level of a warning siren in my family that I finally got the message.

In essence, the message said that our family needed to make some changes. We would not absorb the full impact of the situation for many more months; yet, as the process unfolded, we began to realize that the way our family functioned was the result of the influence of several families and dozens of people and many experiences in the backgrounds of both my wife and myself. Many of those methods of functioning were unacceptable to our children and so, by extension, were unacceptable to my wife and me as well. How we behaved and thought had taken at least two generations to develop; rethinking and restructuring the way we lived would take a long time. But we had no choice if we wanted our family to be fulfilling for all four of us. Like every other family, we had a wealth of internal resources.

When we examined ourselves, these were the resources that we identified: our concern for one another, our commitment to improvement and change, our own intelligence and thought processes and verbal skills (necessary for good communication), and a basic theological orientation that provided hope. A will to change and to grow is half the journey, but not necessarily the most difficult half. We also realized that even with the qualities we brought to our difficulties, we still would have to seek outside help in order to learn how to use what we had.

Our first outside resource proved to be a seminary classmate and friend of mine who was a pastoral counselor. (A "pastoral counselor" is a seminary-trained, ordained member of the clergy who is also trained and licensed in some areas of psychotherapy.) Our entire family agreed to work with him because we believed that ours was a "family" problem or need. We chose not to focus attention solely upon Portia as the "one with the problem." In fact, she was less the problem than her parents, although her parents were very slow to realize that painful truth.

Our counselor knew immediately where to begin. He guided us with the gentleness of a friend and the skill of one well-trained and vastly experienced. So, for the next few months, during which we saw a series of other counselors and eventually physicians, we engaged ourselves in the difficult task of learning to relate to one another differently than we had during all the years of our daughters' growing up. Progress was slow, and the pain of changing was enormous, but little by little we were able to draw less upon outside experts and more upon our own family resources.

As I look back to the beginnings of our process, I realize how initially desperate we were for help. We were afraid for Portia and devoid of any confidence in ourselves. We needed professional reassurance and guidance to be able to use our own family skills and personal strengths. The fact that some things were not working for us did not mean that we had nothing of value and no skills to apply to our problems.

As we began to make progress and as our perceptions began to clear, we became increasingly aware of both our weaknesses and our skills as a family; we also discovered the unevenness in quality among professionals who work with teenagers and families. On the one hand, we discovered a high-school guidance counselor who was as competent and compassionate as anyone for whose services we paid. On the other hand, we discovered an inexcusable lack of professionalism on the part of a significant number of public school teachers, some of whom contributed fantastic rumors about the reasons for Portia's extended absence from school. We found still other teachers to be surprisingly disinterested in her situation and even resentful of the inconvenience of having to provide information about homework for the classes she missed. Most, however, were caring and involved. Those who responded personally and directly became resource people for all of us over the next two years. A few of these individuals have remained involved in Portia's life, and have taken careful interest in Jessica during her high-school career.

We also discovered that counselors and physicians were not all equally competent. One family counselor maintained a perfect balance between professional distance and compassion, between his own responsibilities and those we as a family had to accept. Another proved to be so locked in to a particular clinical methodology that he never made a helpful therapeutic connection with Portia. One psychiatrist was completely devoid of compassion and made no contribution at all to our progress. One physician brushed aside Portia's inquiry about a physical problem — a problem that proved to be one of the major factors in her depression. Finding the right professionals was an ongoing struggle, but we were committed to growth, and we applied the same intensity to the effort that we had applied to all our other best intentions through the years.

In the process of our work with various professionals, I began to suspect that the one area in which no progress was being made was neither relational nor psychological but physical. I telephoned our family physician and told him about my suspicion, mentioning that Portia's complaints had been brushed aside, trivialized by another medical specialist. He quickly sent us to the head of a department at a major teaching hospital. At the exact time of the appointment, the doctor came to the waiting room, introduced himself, and asked for a few minutes to review the charts we had brought along. He then returned and asked to see Portia alone. Later he called me into the office so I could listen to his assessment. He talked to her and not to me, explaining her problem and his recommendations. As Portia and I left his office and walked to the car, she turned to me and said, "Dad, I've finally found a real doctor!" He was real because he took her seriously, and because he knew what he was doing in the area of the human body. He identified a physical problem and confirmed the depressing effect of a medication she had taken. Without providing us an excuse for our family problems, he had given us help with a major contributor to Portia's depression.

All this is meant to suggest that the decision to seek professional help — psychological and medical — does not guarantee that we will immediately find the perfect physician or counselor. If we as parents have looked within ourselves to determine if we are indeed willing to change, and if we are honestly willing to do the hard work required in that process, the next step will be to find the professionals who can help us. Not all are equally competent, skilled, and sensitive. Even some who exhibit all three of these qualities may not be as good a match for us as certain others. If, after reasonable time and effort, we're not satisfied with the progress we're making with certain professionals, we do well to look elsewhere for assistance.

At this juncture it is appropriate to say something about how the clergy can help troubled families. I see these professionals both as peers and as colleagues, but I also see them from the vantage point of parents who seek their assistance. Few pastors are trained counselors. Yet, families for whom faith is vital and formative often turn first to their ministers. Because family and faith are so tightly bound together, problems in our families often cause us to suspect that something is wrong with our belief system. What have we done to be punished like this? Where is God when we need God most? How can we deal with our pain, shame, failure, and loss?

Now, speaking less as a parent and more as a practicing clergyman, I offer these suggestions relating to the clergy as part of our resource system.

The traumas and crises that are often a part of the teen years require spiritual resources. Given the value that Christians place upon persons and the family, confession and repentance and forgiveness, the providence of God and hope, the community of faith, it is natural that we feel a strong need for the clergy when our family patterns are upset. I try to respond to such needs in the congregation I serve.

Nevertheless, I recognize the limits of my training and my schedule. I tell parents, teenagers, and families that I will consult with them as pastor but not as therapist. Instead, I am always prepared to suggest to them a significant number and range of people who could help them. I tell them in detail about each counselor and physician I suggest, giving them several choices based upon the personality, training, and methodology of those individuals. My role subsequently becomes that of spiritual support person, encourager, and interpreter.

Unfortunately, many of the clergy attempt to do more for families than they are trained to do; the result is often simplistic approaches that in the long run cause more distress than they alleviate. Ministers, like other professionals, are not equally gifted, so the usefulness of their counsel and their referrals will vary widely. Consequently, a family will need to assess the helpfulness of their minister in dealing with a given problem in much the same way they assess the helpfulness of other professionals.

The primary role of the clergy person seems to me to be that of priest — offering prayers, hearing confessions, and modeling the presence and grace of God. An additional role will be that of theologian — struggling with major "why" questions. And, of course, the minister will also serve in the role of fellow pilgrim on the human journey. The long-term and specific work of analysis and restructuring of the family's function should be turned over to those trained specifically for such work. It may be, however, that a parish minister is trained and credentialed in such areas as marriage and family counseling; if so, he or she should be evaluated and chosen by the same standards we apply to all other such professionals. Fee considerations should also be discussed with such clergy, just as they would be with counselors in private practice. And that raises one of the more difficult issues for families seeking help — the cost.

Perhaps the most alarming aspect of the helping process proves to be the cost. Hours of talk therapy, various psychological evaluations, physical assessments and medications — all over a period of many months — can end up costing thousands of dollars. Fortunately, many health insurance plans assist families with these expenses, and government-sponsored or private counseling centers offer assistance on a sliding-fee-scale basis. When money is a problem, families may be required to search more diligently for professionals whose services are offered through these programs of assistance.

For families with troubled adolescents, the most costly (and controversial!) aspect of the helping network is the in-patient programs offered by various hospitals. Such in-patient care should be a choice of last resort. Of course, if a teenager has lost touch with reality, is out of control, and is a threat to himself or herself and/or others, this may be a necessity rather than an option. Unfortunately, as parents have become increasingly frustrated with the complications of the growing-up process, and as professionals have chosen to pass on to others their most difficult cases, in-patient treatment has become increasingly popular. In many cases the most positive effect appears to be the therapy of distance — a period of separation that allows everyone in the family a kind of time out. Not infrequently, however, a foster-care arrangement could have provided the same benefits at a much lower cost. Both families and mental health professionals should consider very carefully the necessity, the value, and the cost of such hospitalization, reviewing and eliminating other alternatives until in-patient therapy remains the only option.

On the positive side of the in-patient issue is surely the variety of resources available in one place. Psychiatrists, social workers, physicians, family therapists, substance abuse counselors, and chaplains can be consulted. Individual therapy, family therapy, group therapy of all sorts, and many aftercare options also make these programs attractive. The question I continue to ask about choosing in-patient care is whether or not it indicates that we as families are looking for a quick solution to problems that have taken years to develop, and that we are really looking for someone else to do our work for us. Each family must answer that question for itself. Several years removed from my family's experience with such a program, I remain ambivalent.

Besides the family's own internal resources and the network of professionals, another resource deserves mention: the community of extended family and friends. This resource has already been discussed in detail in an earlier chapter. Suffice it to say at this point that many of our relatives, neighbors, and friends have undergone the same struggles we are experiencing; some are dealing simultaneously with the same issues we are facing. These people often stand ready to listen, to serve as nonauthoritative adult friends to our teenagers, and to do many of the routine things necessary to keep our households going while we work on family issues. Parents trying to learn and grow in the midst of their adolescents' turmoils do well to confide in these friends and accept their assistance and support. These are times when our instincts may tell us to turn inward because of our feelings of failure and shame. The last emotion we need to deal with, however, is loneliness. I will always be grateful for those friends who cared about us in quiet ways — some whom we asked to help, and a few who just appeared, unbidden.

What I Wish I Had Known

Always the struggle with crises in parenting involves guilt, questioning, and self-doubts. As I think back on more than two decades as a parent, I realize that I have no desire to go back and do it all over again. I doubt if I would do a better job even if I knew then what I know now; a different set of problems and needs would present themselves. Yet, because every experience carries with it the potential to help us grow in all other areas of our lives, I continue to speculate about knowledge, skills, and maturity I wish I had possessed when our children were born. These are things that I have become increasingly aware of in the process of parenting, and they are proving valuable to my life even as my primary parenting years draw to a close.

I would suggest that parents just beginning their journey focus on four things: a knowledge of personality makeup, an understanding of "family systems," the ability to balance enjoyment and work in parenting (and in whatever else we do!), and the need to make steady progress in the marital relationship.

First, personality types. I wish I had known more about the human personality and how each of us functions in the family not so much according to choice but according to what we bring into life at birth. I discovered much of this because crisis forced me to grope for reasons why my efforts at parenting were no longer working. Our counselors steered us toward these insights. Two particular profiles of human temperament proved to be significant for my family: "The Bi-Polar Analysis of Core Strengths" and the "Myers/Briggs Personality Inventory." Each of these relatively inexpensive profiles of personality types opened important windows for me and my family, teaching us a great deal about our essential natures as individuals. Three of us are basically quiet, private persons, and one is outgoing, people-and-activity-oriented. Three of us tend to be conservative by nature; the other is a risk-taker, an experimenter. We discovered the extent to which each of us is either a dreamer/planner or a detail person. We explored the extent to which each of us emphasizes feeling and/or thinking. The list of characteristics includes eight aspects/strengths, and the degree to which each is dominant or secondary.

These profiles enabled us to understand how each of us functions and relates. In a very real sense, we found some quasi-scientific permission to be who we are, and some additional bases on which we could relate to one another in more accepting and supportive ways. Many of Portia's struggles became clearer to us when we realized for the first time how different her personality is from those of the other three of us — and how she contributed a balance of humor, risk, and socialization to our family. As the self-appointed "molder and shaper" of personhood, I had unwittingly tried to direct her toward interests and behavior patterns completely opposite those toward which her temperament called her. As a consequence, she was forced to fight (the battle image again!) to be who she is. All of us experienced a high degree of frustration in the process. But all of us have learned a great deal from the upheaval, and the reward has been a much better understanding of each of our personalities and how each of us expresses that personality.

Another "discovery" involved what is known as "family systems." Because my wife, now a licensed professional counselor, had been a college psychology major and was at the beginning of our family crisis a graduate student in counseling, she had done a significant amount of reading in this area. I was simultaneously gaining some understanding of family systems through my professional reading. When our family became "clients," we began to look carefully at our own "genograms" — those charts that look like family trees and are designed to help us see patterns of behavior and relationships in our families of origin and in our own nuclear families. We began to realize that some areas of dysfunction in our own nuclear family were ones that my wife and I had brought along with us from our childhood families. When those patterns of behavior no longer "worked," and we understood the reasons, we were willing to accept the fact that some major changes were mandatory.

I mention these rather technical and complex behavioral theories in order to suggest that families in crisis can be given the tools, the structure, and the understanding to help themselves. Therapists who work with family systems and methodologies and/or theories of temperament/personality can produce important mirrors by which troubled families can see themselves more clearly. The result will be not so much a series of chastisements for where they have gone wrong as a series of revelations about their strengths and how they complement the entire family. I think about how much richer our family might have been if we had understood and encouraged Portia's personality; she would have brought far more humor, risk, color, and high adventure to our rather staid and traditional patterns of living. Now, since we have come to such understanding, she is much freer to express who she really is, and we find her contributions positively unsettling. The gifts she has given us have been much needed.

I wish I had discovered these realities of the human personality and family systems two or three decades earlier. But since my family and I have so much of our lives still ahead, those discoveries will continue to contribute to our growth as persons and as a family.

The third category of those things I wish I had known or done differently has to do with the investment of energy — the balance between enjoyment and work. I frequently find myself talking with parents of very small children, sharing in their optimism and joy — but with the guardedness of one who has also known failure and disillusionment. On one such occasion I found myself sitting in a rocking chair in a maternity ward, holding a newborn child and talking in a rather grandfatherly vein to the parents. I think holding the infant took me back through the years to the births of my own daughters. As I rocked and talked, I heard myself wishing that I had not tried so hard, worked so hard, been so determined during those preschool years. I wish I had worried less about doing everything "right" and teaching them as much as possible and introducing them to every imaginable experience in life.

They would have been happier — and so would I — had I simply allowed them to explore and discover, ask the questions before I answered them, solve problems as they came to them. I would have been far more "effective" as a parent if I had been more affirming, more celebrative, more playful. I wish I had made parenting more of a celebration and less of a project! The heart of the wish? To have enjoyed them as preschoolers, to have allowed them to take more of the lead as school-aged children, and to have invested my working energy toward the adolescent tasks.

In short, I would have read almost nothing about parenting infants and preschoolers, instead of the dozens of volumes I pored over. I may have looked into the developmental stages of children, but not with much fervor. I would have invested myself in enjoyment, play, and celebration. But when Portia reached puberty, I would have sought every book available on the subject of adolescence, and I would have studied them all like a scholar. I would have attended as many workshops as possible designed to help parents of adolescents. I would have used my energy when it would have counted most. As it was, I think I wore myself out being a good parent of small children; by the time they became adolescents, my pride in perfection had reached a shameful level, and my energy had been used up. I had set myself up for mediocrity. When I saw in the mirror of my children what I had done, the revelation proved painful beyond imagination.

As circumstances dictated, however, I ended up investing even greater amounts of energy in learning, changing, and growing during our children's adolescence. In the long term, these investments in growth will benefit all of us, and perhaps the next generation of adolescents in our family.

The final thing I wish I had done differently is the most important one: I wish I had invested more heavily in my marriage. This is not to say that the marriage was necessarily bad, nor is it to suggest that it was even weak. It is meant to underscore the reality that the best gift parents can give their children is to be a happy, growing couple. In our first ten years of marriage, my wife and I never looked closely at how we made decisions, managed conflict, expressed intimacy, or even communicated. We were both busy with our own careers, assuming that everything about the marriage was working. When the children were born, we were too busy watching them, teaching them, and trying to be perfect parents; we had little time, energy, or inclination to look at each other and our individual needs.

But very little growth was taking place in our marriage. We were both heavily involved in graduate school and work, and neither of us was listening very well to the other. Neither of us had worked through our attitudes toward and understanding of our families of origin, or through several losses and griefs, or through our own expectations of each other or even of life itself. Of course, we readily admit, few young people at age thirty (which is how old we were when Portia was born) have all those issues worked out; nor do many more at age forty or so (which is how old we were when Portia's puberty began). Nevertheless, I was so focused on things outside myself, and perhaps my wife was as well, that we were making no progress in our relationship. Periodic flashes of discontent and hints of the absence of growth in our marriage were easy to slough off or ignore completely. And so we did! At least until Portia forced us to examine everything connected with our family. That process is now ongoing, as it should have been twenty years earlier.

The title of this chapter is "Where To Go for Help." The title might well be broadened to include "When To Go for Help." For my wife and me, the answer would be that we would have done well to have explored who we were and how we were relating even before our first child was born. Much of the help we searched out in our daughters' teen years would have been unnecessary if we had sought it years earlier. The old adage that says "If it ain't broke, don't fix it" tends to cause too many of us to think in terms of marriage as brokenness and repair rather than as a journey in relationship. Our marriage was not broken, nor did it need repair. Our relationship as a journey, however, was static, and lacked vitality. We needed to nurture a growing relationship, and ours was neither growing nor being nurtured.

For parents committed to excellence, the first among several priorities is surely a vital and growing relationship with one another. When parents are not clear about who they are and do not clearly understand their own personalities and family backgrounds, they will tend to be less able to understand their own children and to allow them to be who they are; thus the family unit will be less able to function well. When parents are unable to state clearly to one another their own personal needs, they will be less able to hear their children or to allow them to state their needs. When parents are unable to differentiate themselves within the marriage and in their other relationships, they will have difficulty allowing their children to declare their own uniqueness. When parents are unable to express intimacy in a variety of celebrative ways, they will have difficulty expressing intimacy to their children and accepting expressions of intimacy from them, especially when those children become adolescents.

Where do young married adults go to find marital help? A variety of excellent marriage enrichment programs are available and inexpensive. Self-help books abound. Many ministers and counselors provide direction, advice, and resources. The best beginning point I know is to learn about personality and temperament types and family systems. Couples can explore these areas together and follow them as far as they have the need, inclination, and energy. Such an approach focuses attention upon the journey, upon strengths, and upon growth; whatever is malfunctioning can be dealt with in the context of affirmation rather than deficiency.

I wish I had known much earlier about personality types and core strengths and family systems. I wish I had known that adolescence would be the time in childhood development that requires the most energy and attention. And I wish I had known how important it is for the parents of growing children to have a growing marriage. Nevertheless, if a parent, like me, has limitations in these areas, they are not destructive if at some point or points along the way they are recognized and dealt with. And the growing, changing, and learning process will continue to benefit us long after our children are grown. If we as parents struggle to grow, we offer a lifetime model for our own children to do the same.

Conclusion

Some Reflections about Failure and Success

WITH one daughter in her early twenties and the other in her late teens, my role as a parent is now drastically altered. I no longer have primary responsibility for the well-being of either girl, although I suspect I lost that much sooner than I thought I did! Even though one daughter has completed college and the other is midway through that part of her journey, what I contribute in financial and relational support is only a part of the "responsibility network" they have formed. One works full-time and the other works part-time, contributing significantly to their increasing self-sufficiency. They both possess a solid network of friends in all age categories. They both must and do make their own decisions about most issues.

The shift from parent-with-primary-responsibility to parent learning adult-to-adult ways of relating has been slow and painful. The girls have wanted that shift to occur sooner and more quickly than I thought was best for them and/or was prepared to allow. Their haste to test their wings has led to several severe falls and all the bruises that accompany such slips. Theirs were not so much rebellious desires to get out from under my protection, control, or domination as normal adolescent desires to explore, discover, and test their own perceptions. The pain their decisions often inflicted upon them and their parents has been real and at times excruciating. The joys we experience in their progress, however, are balancing the pain.

The years ahead will be a period of assessment for me. I sometimes envy those whose personalities enable them to accept what they have done as a mix of good and bad, and then move on without self-blame or recrimination, or even much analysis. I am a different sort of person. Even though I cannot go back and redo anything, I grow and learn by analysis and assessment of what I have done. Because I am at heart a teacher and a fellow pilgrim, I must share my discoveries both as a gift and as a means to test them.

I have mentioned many things I would have done differently, and I have readily recognized some mistakes I have made in relating to my family. The girls now have the enormous task of sorting out their own personality types, their family system, and their theories of relating to others — and perhaps someday those "others" will include children. If the first couple of decades have been marked by my own mediocrity as a parent, what about the next two?

I hope that I will mind my own business, allow the girls the privilege of trial and error, wait for questions before offering answers, be quick with affirmation and slow with suggestions, and offer financial help only when it is truly necessary or positive in its contribution to their actual well-being. I hope that I will be possessed of more good humor and less intensity than I was in those years before the sharp edges of my personality were blunted by crisis.

The loss of innocence inflicts one kind of pain on the young, another kind on the middle-aged. The young cry and subsequently protect themselves a bit better and avoid people and situations they no longer trust, but they charge ahead with unflagging energy and optimism. To us older folk, they seem to have short memories. But there is at least a second loss of innocence which we experience as we grow older that is much different. The years chip away at the unqualified trust we placed in people and institutions, but we attempt to preserve a certain innocence about private values — especially as they relate to family, work, and religion. When those core values are battered, however, the airy kind of optimism that allows the young to cry a while and then charge ahead is gone; we adults are sometimes stopped in our tracks. But the substance of support comes from a source deeper than optimism, and that source is hope.

At the time that our family began to descend into the crises we experienced in Portia's adolescence, my wife and I had been charging ahead in youthful optimism. We could do anything. We never got really tired. We never ran out of ideas and answers. But when we feared for Portia's life and began the discovery of our girls' entanglements, we examined closely for the first time how we did things, and we discovered the error of some of our ways. This second loss of innocence — the loss of those private values concerning family, work, and religion — rendered "charging ahead" a dead option.

A certain sadness descended on me. I was depressed and grieving about what I had lost — never mind that I needed to lose much of it if I was to grow as a person. Very slowly, however, a deep level of hope began to replace that airy optimism of my own young adult years. Gradually I have become better able to choose when I will be directly involved and subjective in my analysis, and when I will stand back and watch with some objectivity. I tend to be much less certain about most things, but more solidly confident about a few things that matter most to me.

In a real sense, the adolescent years of our daughters have been adolescent years for me as well. During that time I have tried to complete some parts of those four adolescent tasks that I had not finished in my early twenties. But these tasks are somewhat like wisdom teeth: the longer one waits to take care of them, the more discomfort one feels! The healing has been slow and painful, but I expect the results to be very good.

What can be said in summary, then, about mediocrity? First, such an evaluation is more a matter of feelings than of scientific analysis. What exactly is an excellent parent? If I make an assessment today of the job I have done, I might be kinder to myself than if I had made the assessment five years ago. If my family offers an opinion today, it might change twenty years from now. Further, such evaluations are always made in relation to some kind of standards, goals, and expectations. My standards were unrealistically high, almost arrogant. Given the small amount of actual control any parent has over genes and chromosomes, personality types, and the influence of our culture, judging the quality of parenting is difficult: what is mediocrity to me may appear to be excellence to others, or total failure to still others. I only know that on the one hand I feel relatively sad about my perceived shortcomings as a parent, whereas on the other hand I am pleased with my growth as a person.

One factor remains to be underscored about parenting: the will of the children themselves. Babies are not blank slates upon which all-wise parents write. They are not formless masses of clay that parents shape into some relatively beautiful sculptures. Neither are they blocks of fine wood to be crafted into some "useful" things. Even with the best or worst a parent is or does, a child is a person in his or her own right and will have a great deal to say about what appears to be the success or failure of parents. When a youngster turns out to be an exceptional person, who can say how much the parents or the teachers or the clergy or the neighbors or even the television industry contributed to that excellence? Taking credit or blame falls into the "easy" category!

Our daughters grew up with an enviable array of advantages, not the least of which is above-average intelligence. They have constantly been making choices since their earliest years. I must and do accept some responsibility for the tools and models I was able to provide for them; I have recently begun to accept less and less responsibility — actual and imagined — for their decisions. Even those poor decisions they made several years ago, those decisions I was certain were the result of my failures as a parent, now seem to me more a matter of shared responsibilities. Perhaps some of them have absolutely nothing to do with me. I find it less and less important to place blame, and more and more important to grow in whatever experiences are theirs, mine, and ours.

As parents we do well to recognize very early that we deserve neither blame for everything our children do wrong, nor praise for everything they do well. We do even better to accept the fact that society may see our children as a reflection of our quality as persons, our competence as parents, and even our worth as human beings. In truth, our children reflect something of us as parents, but they are not the sole measurement of our identity, competence, or value.

Our daughters' adolescent years have been intense and difficult for them and for our family. (I suspect the overwhelming majority of families would readily admit the same about their own experiences of these years.)

They have been growing years for all four of us. We have worked together in that growth while maintaining our extensive responsibilities in our academic pursuits, our work, our social lives, and our church. I am still a parent, but my daughters are not so much children now as they are adults with whom I choose to relate as adults. I am finding that relationship increasingly laden with rewards — not in small part because of the battles we have traded for consultation and negotiation. Success and failure, winning and losing, good and bad — such things are far less important these days than the shared journey. And that is more and more a celebration!

Afterword

PORTIA B. PRICE

LIVING in the Price family was not easy for me as a young child. My parents did their best to make sure both my sister and I knew we were loved. We were never permitted to have everything we wanted, but we always had everything we needed . . . or so my parents believed. What none of us knew then was that many of my needs were and are different from theirs; these were the needs that went unfulfilled.

I always needed to be around people; my parents were introverts of the purest sort. I seemed never to like to do things the way other people — especially my parents — did them. I wanted to create my own more innovative ways to do ordinary, simple tasks; this purposeful complication bewildered my "do-it-simply" parents. When I was a child, I wanted very much to join all the activities my friends joined and wear the name-label clothes they all seemed to have; my Mom and Dad wanted me to be "different" from whatever happened to be the norm.

During my adolescent years, I chose to be "different," but not in the ways my parents approved of. My desire to be perceived as unique manifested itself in ways that alienated people; many thought I was more weird than one-of-a-kind. In my early teen years, I wore unusual clothing and had my hair cut in odd styles and colored in every hue except my natural color. I endured the most agonizing alienation imaginable. I felt separated from society, from school, from my family, and most of all from myself. At the time I was sure I knew who I was, and I claimed to express my true self in my outward appearance and by the friends I chose. As I reflect upon those efforts, I now realize I had absolutely no idea who I was. All my efforts at self-expression were in reality a part of my search for my self.

At the beginning of my senior year in high school, I was still bleaching my naturally brunette hair blond, but I had begun to wear more traditional clothing and to cut my hair in a more conservative manner. I gradually began to "grow into myself" and out of the "I must be different" stage. I told my parents that the only thing I had yet to change in order to be my natural self was my blond hair; the day they saw me with my own hair color would be the day they would know I had decided to begin growing up. It was not long after that pronouncement that I made the decision to allow my natural hair color to grow out. I cried when I made the decision because I was giving up a part of myself that had been so much of my identity for so long a time.

As teenagers grow older, they begin to struggle with the fact that maturity demands that they must take increased responsibility for who they become. Coming to this realization is threatening because they recognize that they must accept responsibility for their own mistakes. During this period teenagers must also deal with their parents' humanity. Everything they were taught under the authority of "because I told you so" is shattered. Gradually they come to see Mom and Dad as just people, people who make mistakes, and they discover that their parents' ways of thinking and doing things may not be acceptable to them. Still, they may be afraid not to follow their parents' value systems and opinions. Teenagers also begin to realize how their parents may have made mistakes in raising them. They may become confused or even angry when they think of themselves as having been experiments of their parents; yet every child is in a sense a parent's experiment. No parent is an expert at raising children, and each child brings his or her own set of problems and situations to the relationship. Parents do what they believe is right and best; they hope their efforts will turn out well. The end result, however, may be different from what the parents had expected. They do well to prepare themselves for some disappointments.

My mother and father still grieve about all the mistakes they made and occasionally express their sorrow. I dislike hearing those expressions because it seems to me that they wish I were a better person. It makes me feel as if I have failed. So I must remind them once in a while that I really have turned out wonderfully. I am neither sad nor sorry about who I am or about whatever mistakes may have been made in my childhood. None of us knew then as much as we know now. We have committed ourselves, however, to allowing the mistakes to remain in the past and to living in as loving a manner as possible.

Appendix A: Signs of Problems
in Adolescent Adjustment

MOST adolescents undergo normal mood and behavior swings as part of the physical transformation they experience. But more serious changes in attitude and behavior should serve as warning signs that their adjustment is not going well. These signs are listed below in two sections. The first group lists several signs, any one of which may indicate no problem beyond the normal adjustment process, but any two or more of which, if they appear together, sound an alarm. The second group includes those signs any one of which clearly indicates a problem.

GROUP I

- Changes in eating and sleeping habits
- Withdrawing/silence
- Nightmares

- Dramatic shifts in behavior patterns
- Choosing friends of a much different kind than in the past
- A series of broken relationships
- A decline in academic performance/interest in school
- Feigned illnesses
- Challenging/breaking minor household rules
- Wearing clothing more bizarre than different

GROUP II

- Talk of death/suicide
- Fighting with other young people
- Sexual promiscuity
- Running away from home
- Substance use/abuse
- Violation of major household rules
- Trouble with the law
  - Arrest for substance abuse
  - Driving under the influence
  - Shoplifting/stealing
  - School truancy
  - A series of traffic violations
- Suicide gestures/attempts

Appendix B: Helpful Groups and Programs

THE following groups and programs are all national in scope. The specific meeting arrangements and details for a particular city or area can be gotten by calling the group/program listing in the phone book, by getting in touch with mental health centers in larger towns and cities, or by contacting school guidance counselors.

- Tough Love
- Systematic Training for Effective Parenting (STEP)
- Active Parenting (offered by schools)
- Families Anonymous
- Adolescent Parent Support Group
- Child-Parent Support Group (offered at some psychiatric hospitals)

Selected Bibliography

Curran, Dolores. *Traits of a Healthy Family: Fifteen Traits Found in Healthy Families by Those Who Work with Them*. Minneapolis: Winston Press, 1983.

As the title indicates, Curran explores those traits that are characteristic of healthy families and offers practical suggestions for families to follow.

Dobson, James. *Hide or Seek*. Old Tappan, N.J.: Fleming H. Revell, 1974.

In this book Dobson provides an excellent description of the adolescent's egocentric perception that he or she is ugly and dumb. Understanding this mind-set helps parents better understand an adolescent's reactive behaviors.

SELECTED BIBLIOGRAPHY

Elkind, David. *The Hurried Child: Growing Up Too Fast Too Soon*. Reading, Mass.: Addison-Wesley Publishing Co., 1981.

This book is helpful to parents because it explains the unrealistic cultural expectations placed on children and how these expectations influence their decision making.

——. *All Grown Up and No Place to Go: Teenagers in Crisis*. Reading, Mass.: Addison-Wesley Publishing Co., 1984.

Building on *The Hurried Child*, Elkind here explores the difficulties teenagers face in a society preoccupied with instant gratification and materialism.

Gardner, James E. *The Turbulent Teens: Understanding, Helping, Surviving*. San Diego: Oak Tree Publications, 1983.

In this readable, anecdotal book, Gardner uses case histories to focus on the adolescent issues of sex, drugs, and alcohol use, and offers parents practical ways to deal with these issues.

Gardner, Richard A. *Understanding Children: A Parents' Guide to Child Rearing*. Cresskill, N.J.: Creative Therapeutics, 1979.

Gardner, a well-known child psychologist and play therapist, offers practical suggestions for disciplining children.

156

SELECTED BIBLIOGRAPHY

Kaplan, Louise. *Adolescence: A Farewell to Childhood*. New York: Simon & Schuster, 1984.

This is an insightful, well-researched study (more theoretical than some) of adolescent behavior that looks at the consequences of some of the hazards of adolescent development (e.g., teenage pregnancy, drug use, alcohol abuse, parental abuse).

Lickona, Thomas. *Raising Good Children: Helping Your Child Through the Stages of Moral Development*. New York: Bantam, 1983.

This is a superlative study of the moral development of children and adolescents that examines this development by stages.

Littwin, Susan. *The Postponed Generation: Why America's Grown-Up Kids Are Growing Up Later*. Ed. Pat Golbitz. New York: William Morrow, 1986.

A study of the effects of the permissive parenting of the last generation and its implications for youth.

Strommen, Merton. *Five Cries of Youth*. New York: Harper & Row, 1988.

Strommen discusses some of the issues adolescents face and some of the practical needs they have.

York, Phyllis; David York; and Ted Wachtel. *Toughlove*. New York: Doubleday, 1982.

———. *Toughlove Solutions*. New York: Doubleday, 1984.

These books are not for the fainthearted. They take tough stands on dealing with the hazards of adolescent development (teenage pregnancy, drug use, alcohol abuse, parental abuse). Both books propose a supportive approach involving all those who have a relationship with and care about the young person.